THE TIMES
AVIATORS

THE TIMES

AVIATORS

A HISTORY IN PHOTOGRAPHS

Michael J. H. Taylor

Collins

An Imprint of HarperCollinsPublishers

ISBN-10:0–00–716124–7
ISBN-13:978–0–00–716124–9

ISBN-10:0–06–081906–5 (in the United States)
ISBN-13:978–0–06–081906–4

Color separations by Colourscan, Singapore
Printed and bound in Italy by Editoriale Johnson

10 09 08 07 06 05
9 8 7 6 5 4 3 2 1

Acknowledgements
Michael Taylor wishes to thank Philip Jarrett for his contributions to parts of Chapters 2 and 3, on the work of Hargrave, Lilienthal, Mozhaiskii, Pilcher, Whitehead, and others. Also, thanks go out to Bill Gunston for his timely contributions to Chapter 7, on World War II. The publishers would additionally like to thank: Thomas Cussans; Brian Riddle, RAeS; F. W. Armstrong, RAeS; Mark Wagner and Mark Steele, aviation-images.com; Austin J. Brown and Jim Winchester, The Aviation Picture Library; Ted Nevill, TRH Pictures.

Contents

Foreword

When this book was planned, it was agreed that it should not be merely another typical aviation history. The quality and uniqueness of the photographs available, the new depths of research made possible by the opening of archives in the former Soviet Union, for example, and the latest insights into, and interpretation of, events from the past all permitted a freedom to produce something a little special.

By the standards of some encyclopaedic volumes on aviation history, where many hundreds of thousands of words printed on a thousand pages permit the broadest discourse on every facet of aviation, this book has neither the space nor the remit to be so comprehensive. Instead, its real strength lies in its ability to provide a modern overview from which the reader may become enthused to search out further information on particular areas of interest, seen initially in the wider context through the text written here. What is certain is that aviation and aviation history never stand still: they are evolving continuously. Adventurers plan new ways of getting into the history books, designers seek out new convenient and economic means to improve air travel, and safety is meeting such exacting standards that it may be thought that ground-based forms of transport are, in comparison, positively dangerous. In the military field it seems that almost anything is possible, and the strangest shapes and shadows in the sky are proof that imagination and hardware can sometimes go hand in glove.

How long has aviation been around? Some might say one hundred years, because 17 December 2003 marks the one hundredth anniversary of Orville Wright's first 12-second powered flight, and everybody has heard of the Wright brothers. This 'sacred cow' of history is all very well, but it is not being irreverent to the memory and achievements of the Wrights to say that this is, in truth, incorrect without first adding specific qualifications as to the standards that should be met before claiming a true flight.

There are many other examples of 'headline' history that hide the wider picture, requiring further examination to get at the underlying facts. For example, the aeronautical designs of Leonardo da Vinci may be seen as less progressive than at first thought when viewed within the context of the work of other contemporary and lesser known persons. Similarly, and many centuries later, it is often wrongly stated that the two atomic bombs dropped on Japan in 1945 brought an immediate and apocalyptic end to the World War II. Not so. Five days after the B-29 bomber *Bock's Car* attacked Nagasaki with the second operational atomic bomb in the USAAF inventory, more than 900 B-29s and fighters carried out further 'conventional' attacks on Japan that brought matters to a final head. And, in more recent times, it is often overlooked that the USSR put the first supersonic airliner into commercial use. This, the Tupolev Tu-144, beat the ultimately much more successful Anglo-French Corcorde by a month, carrying freight and mail ahead of Concorde's historic, and much more relevant, passenger-carrying operations commencing in early 1976.

History is so often a matter of interpretation and it is vital to search beneath the headlines to try to gain a complete and accurate understanding of past events.

Michael Taylor, 2003

Flight – the Dream of Ages

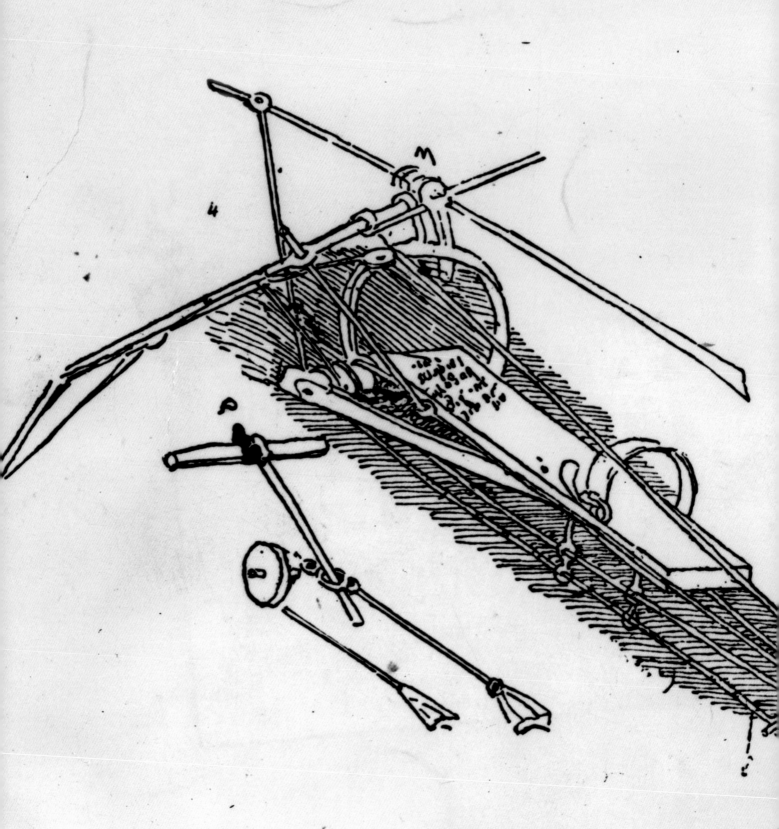

Fig. 4. — Croquis

Léonard de Vinci.

previous spread
Leonardo da Vinci's fascination for heavier-than-air
flight was not matched by any real understanding of
how it could be achieved mechanically. His ornithopter
envisaged the pilot adopting a prone position, thereby
allowing his leg muscles to transmit power to the
flapping wings via pulleys and cables, so boosting arm
and chest muscles. Also shown are the wing structure
and pilot control method for a glider.

above
Engraving of the goddess
Isis on the sarcophagus
of Ramses III, her vulture
wings symbolizing both
'rising' and maternal
care.

'I SEE THAT LANGLEY HAS HAD HIS FLING AND FAILED. IT SEEMS TO BE OUR TURN
TO THROW NOW, AND I WONDER WHAT OUR LUCK WILL BE.'

These words were spoken by Wilbur Wright, after Langley – his greatest rival
to the number one slot in aviation history – had seen his own powered
aeroplane fail to lift and thereafter drop into the Potomac river in 1903. The
words contained no prophesy of the success that was to come, but rather a
hope that years of careful research and engineering would give him and his
brother, Orville, the favourable outcome that had so obviously eluded the
elderly Professor Samuel Pierpont Langley. What Wilbur and Orville Wright
wanted more than anything else was to be the first people in the world to
achieve, in a powered heavier-than-air machine, a flight that was both
controllable and of a duration that was more than a mere 'hop' into the air.

It was to be the difference between the 'hops' of others and the Wrights'
sustained flights of 17 December 1903 that stole the day, thereby becoming
the benchmark of aviation history. Several powered aeroplanes constructed
by others in various countries of the world had beaten the Wright *Flyer* into
the air, but none had been properly witnessed and documented to have
managed anything other than a brief hop from the ground. By the end of that
day in 1903 the Wrights had flown three more times, the best lasting nearly
a minute: they had fulfilled a dream held sacred by man for thousands of
years. But was this the true beginning of aviation?

THE CONCEPT OF HUMAN FLIGHT is as old as recorded history, and it is within the mythology of ancient
times that the story begins. Not surprisingly, several of the myths and legends of flying relate more to
man enlisting the help of the natural world than to any genuine attempt on his part to construct machines
or contrivances capable of generating lift through totally artificial means. A good example of this is the
well-documented flying legend of Alexander the Great, who was said to have attached griffons to a
basket or seat, and to have persuaded them to lift him into the air by dangling cooked meat above their
heads; to descend, he would lower the meat to coax them downwards.

Similar myths of flight, with men using nothing more technical than tethered eagles, cranes and other
birds as power sources, are plentiful. Yet, from among the strange stories of harnessing nature, or
adopting magic, can be plucked the odd gem of science: for example, the tales of chariots of fire and of
man-carrying clouds and smoke might, for those who are wishing to make the leap of faith, show a
primitive connection between the science of flying and the lifting effects of heat. A step too far? Perhaps,
but it is well documented that an attempt to understand the atmosphere had been made, whereby it
was believed that the atmosphere had three principal levels of air, with a temperate lower level and an
excessively hot upper level sandwiching a cold middle area; the different conflicting levels of temperature
were separated by violent buffer zones producing the various weather conditions. Beneath the layers of

air resided the known areas of earth and water. And so, as ancient and medieval philosophy stated that air, earth, fire and water comprised the elements, it was reasoned that any matter comprising a paramountcy of one element would quite naturally be drawn to the level in which it most belonged. In this way, Aristotle stated that fire would rise upwards, just as earth would demonstrate heaviness and fall.

The ancient Chinese, Greeks and Egyptians are sometimes scorned for not achieving more in aeronautics, given their well-recorded thirst for science and construction. They had the materials, after all: so why had they not even made a simple man-carrying glider or hot-air balloon? The answer is that hindsight is a wonderful thing; and in some civilisations it was believed that flying was for gods and perhaps should not be mimicked by mortal man. But even these explanations tell only half the truth, for there was some genuine research that is so often overlooked by historians, as will be detailed later.

In trying to make a meaningful judgement of ancient writings and engravings with regard to flight, it is not too difficult to separate fact from fiction and to manage to extract some small signs of science from the myths. For example, depictions of Isis from ancient Egypt show her with vulture wings and sacred horns. Although the wings were a symbol of maternal care, Isis is also linked with rising, such as the rising of planets and the coming of dawn, when the earth warmed.

In Europe, the best-known story of all was that of Icarus and Daedalus trying to escape from the Labyrinth in Crete, using wings made from feathers and wax. Only when Icarus foolhardily flew too close to the sun, causing the wax to melt, did he fall to his death, as legend observes. In Greek and Roman iconography there are many images of this father and son double act escaping from imprisonment. Whilst

below

A single-seat Ki Kuang flying chariot with multi-blade paddles, wings and a small sail.

modern science tells us that it is merely myth and that they could not have ascended, some scholars believe that the story was based loosely on true events. If there is any chance of reality, then it could be reasoned that they might have attempted to use, say, home-made hang gliders for descending flight, with partial success, or perhaps they had tried to flap their way to freedom, rather less successfully. Either way, the materials chosen and the methods of construction might have been more justly blamed for failure, rather than any inherent flaw in the concept.

A Chinese myth of flying that dates back well over two millennia, and received considerable notoriety, involved the inhabitants of Ki Kuang, a strange people who are said to have flown readily and regularly in man-made machines. Although the precise designs of the craft vary from engraving to engraving, the common factors were seating in a boat-hull or chariot, circular and multi-blade paddles on each side of the 'carriage', and either small wings and a sail or a larger parachute/sail.

Without continuing to describe dozens more examples of flying myths and legends, it can already be seen that certain basics for flying had indeed been appreciated in ancient times, although without practical application. These included the possibility of constructing machines to fly without any assistance from nature, and the creation of lift through fixed wings and propulsion via blades. Most fascinating is that the 'paddles' of the two-seat version of the Ki Kuang craft look very similar to the primitive propellers fitted to some nineteenth-century aeroplanes.

LIMITED ACTUAL EXPERIMENTATION IN THE ANCIENT WORLD did take place, however, although it is the myths that we more readily remember. Archytas of Tarentum was a Greek mathematician and scientist living in Italy in the first half of the fourth century BC, whose experiments included the construction of a small rig to demonstrate artificial flight. Using a small carved wooden bird attached to a freely moving arm, and perfectly balanced by counterweights, he could make the bird lift when propelled in circular motion by a 'hidden and enclosed' force. Later accounts tell of the use of lamps in the experiment, which perhaps indicates propulsion by steam, hot air or compressed air.

As noteworthy as Archytas's experiments were, China outpaced Europe in matters aeronautical, though only just. While it is all too easy to dismiss the humble kite as unimportant in aeronautical terms, in reality this Chinese invention had an importance that spanned centuries. It is not known for sure who invented the kite, but it is generally attributed to Mo Ti, a philosopher who lived during the years 470–391 BC. Remembered more readily as Mo Tzu, he believed in the simple things of life, based on sharing and universal love. An account of his small wooden kite (that took three years to build — and one day to smash) is recorded.

Kites used for practical purposes date from around 200 BC. Records suggest that in about 206 BC (sometimes given as 169 BC) Chinese General Han Hsin used a kite to gauge the distance between his attacking forces and

below

Aerial bombing of a city was depicted in Walter de Milemete's illuminated manuscript of 1326, showing how fire bombs could be dropped from kites that were flown and controlled from outside the city walls by a determined attacking force.

a besieged city, by flying the kite over the city centre and then measuring the length of the tethering string, while in the sixth century AD Chinese forces passed signals using semaphore kites. In 1326 an illuminated manuscript by Walter de Milemete provided the first depiction of a kite in Europe. This was of the 'pennon' type, a typically Chinese design with the box-kite 'lifting' surfaces made to look like a dragon's head and the trailing body acting as a windsock. But, ominously, the illustration showed the kite carrying a fire bomb over a city.

An unconnected science, that initially produced a weapon – and would, centuries later, also have an impact on manned flight and space exploration – was the invention of the rocket, also of Chinese origin. In 1042 Tseng Kung Liang described rockets used in warfare, these first-generation missiles being fuelled by gunpowder. Nearly two centuries later, in 1232, Mongol armies were repelled from Peiping in China by artillery rocket bombardments.

Europe became aware of war rockets as early as 1258, but the concept was not generally seized

upon as a progressive idea for modern warfare. There were exceptions, however, and these included the use of rockets in 1380 during fighting between Venetian and Genoese forces. Yet, to emphasise the generally slow uptake in Europe, during advances into India in the 1780s British forces suffered several major rebuffs at the hands of defenders armed with iron-cased rockets, initially at Guntur. But, having received a thoroughly fine lesson, matters were put in hand to remedy the situation and Colonel William Congreve began a research programme at the Royal Laboratory in Woolwich, intended to develop an artillery rocket for the British forces. Congreve's 'developed' rocket was put on trial in 1805 and on 8 October 1806, during the Napoleonic Wars, the Royal Navy attacked French ships and the town of Boulogne, 24 of its vessels being armed with rockets. In the following year Copenhagen came under a barrage of 25,000 rockets, each with a 3.25-km range. And this was just the beginning!

Not all rocketry involved the military, however. Being born in Venice in about 1395 meant that Giovanni da Fontana had knowledge of rockets from an early age. Like others in his era, he was inspired to conduct his own experiments. Whilst in his twenties, he had filled tubes with gunpowder and seen them soar skywards. By grouping several tubes into the belly of a model bird or other creature made from wood and paper (and sometimes cloth), he produced truly remarkable rocket-powered flying models, with long tails to keep them upright.

It is quite possible to suggest that Fontana had added a winged creature to his rockets only for visual effect, rather than to test or mimic the aerodynamic effects of surfaces travelling through the air. Though there was more exhibition than experimentation, the serious side of the models was that, when used in conjunction with accurate clocks of his own design or with a trailing cord, they could provide a means of measuring distance.

WITHIN THE HISTORY OF FLIGHT, FONTANA ALSO PROVIDES HIS OWN REMARKABLE REFERENCE to early lighter-than-air experimentation. In his written work *Metrologum de pisce cane et volucre*, Fontana mentions an unknown inventor who had unsuccessfully attempted to fly using a very large pyramid of wooden rings and cloth, under which a man sat and lit a fire of pitch and tallow (or similar). The fire and smoke were intended to make the inside air lighter and rarer than that on the outside, thereby forcing the construction to rise. He also detailed possible reasons for failure, which included too little fire and a structure that was too small or too heavy.

What Fontana had described, as we now know, was an early attempt to produce a hot-air balloon of sorts, albeit conical. Yet, even this wasn't the first reference to 'lightness' through warm air for practical purposes. Albertus Magnus, for example, born in about 1200, suggested that a bladder would be lighter when inflated by warm air from the lungs. In England the Franciscan monk, Roger Bacon (born 1214), believed that a thin metal sphere filled with 'ethereal air' or fire would fly in the atmosphere. Interestingly, in Bacon's book of 1250 entitled *Secrets of Art and Nature*, he refers to the possibility of making a manned flying machine with artificial wings to beat the air, the first genuine reference to an ornithopter known to history.

A different approach to 'lightness' with spheres was suggested by Francesco de Lana-Terzi, a Jesuit priest. In his design of 1670 for a lighter-than-air craft — the first to be properly illustrated and recorded

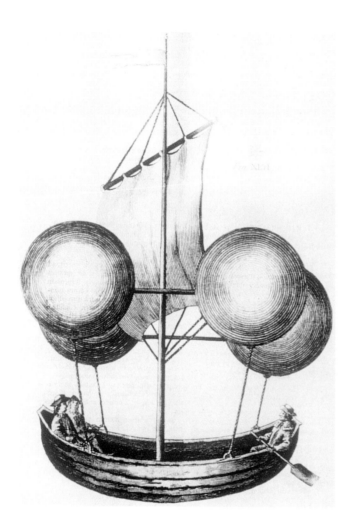

in history – he expected four very thin copper or tin spheres of over 6 m diameter each to be tethered by ropes to a boat hull, producing about 540 kg of lift. To achieve 'lightness', his idea was to extract the air from the spheres, thus creating vacuums. Extraction itself involved filling the raised spheres with water via an opening in the top, whilst a very long tube ran from a tap in the bottom of the sphere into a tank of water. Once full, the top opening would then be closed and made airtight. Using barometric principles, the bottom tap thereafter was opened to vent the water, leaving a vacuum (interestingly, the air pump had been invented by Otto von Guericke and demonstrated 16 years earlier). Spheres without air had to weigh less than spheres containing air, he theorised, and if the spheres weighed less than the displaced air, the spheres would rise.

In practical terms de Lana-Terzi's concept was a non-starter, as the very thinness of the copper or tin would cause the spheres to implode due to the crushing effect of the outside air, among many other insurmountable problems. Nevertheless, he had also envisaged altitude control of his craft, using taps to allow small quantities of air into the spheres, and using ballast, both of which would become effective methods for lighter-than-air craft centuries later. But, on realising his design faults, de Lana-Terzi concluded that God would not allow the invention anyway, citing possible use in warfare.

Such considerations did not deter other religious figures, and it was again in Europe that one of the greatest leaps in aeronautical history took place, although by a Brazilian monk. In 1709 the design for a navigable man-carrying flying machine was published in scientific journals, devised by Father Bartolomeu Laurenço de Gusmão. Named *Passarola*, it was based around a boat hull and adopted large flapping wings and a vertical tail. Above the hull was carried a huge area of cloth, which has since been variously described as a canopy to capture the hot air from a fire, or a parachute for safe descent. Either way, suggestions have more recently been made that the main lifting force was not to have been hot air at all, but a series of rockets. Incredibly, upon de Gusmão's application to King John V of Portugal for a royal privilege, an order was issued on 17 April 1709 forbidding anyone else from trying to construct a similar flying machine.

Clearly the King had great faith in de Gusmão, and duly offered him a professorship of mathematics and a pension for life to continue his work. Such generosity had early pay-back when, on 8 August 1709, de Gusmão demonstrated a model hot-air balloon in the Ambassadors' drawing room at the Casa da India, Lisbon, in the presence of the King, Queen Maria Ann, Cardinal Conti (who later became Pope Innocent III) and many other dignitaries. The small device had every attribute of a modern hot-air balloon; the paper envelope was spherical and was filled with hot air from materials burning in a suspended earthenware bowl.

below

The *Passarola* was a fanciful flying machine design, with little of the practicality found in the August 1709 model hot-air balloon. With flapping wings and a steering tail, it has been a matter of recent conjecture whether hot air captured in the canopy or a series of rockets was to provide the principal lifting force, or, indeed, whether the canopy as intended merely as an emergency parachute.

When released by de Gusmão, the small craft freely floated across the room, eventually rising to 3.5 m above the carpet. Unfortunately, having drifted to the curtains, it had to be beaten to the ground before it set the material ablaze. However, despite the ignominious end, it had been responsible for the first-ever successful demonstration of a hot-air balloon, albeit a model.

It is recorded that de Gusmão produced larger flying machines during August and October that same year, for outside experimentation. It is uncertain whether or not any followed his highly successful model design, but it is possible that he reverted to the impractical *Passarola* layout, as success with a man-carrier eluded him.

below
Painting of the 8 August 1709 model hot-air balloon demonstration in the Ambassador's drawing room at the Casa da India, Lisbon. Rising to 3.5 m, the balloon had to be destroyed by two valets before it set the curtains on fire. King John of Portugal 'was good enough not to take ill.' The hot air came from material burning in a suspended earthenware bowl encrusted in a waxed-wooden tray.

B *Aathe* was by *Bladud* to perfection brought,
By Necromanticke Arts, to flye hee fought:
As from a Towre he thought to fcale the Sky,
He brake his necke, becaufe he foar'd too high.

above

Bladud, the ninth king of Britain, whose reign ended in 843 BC after attempting to fly from a tower in Trinavantum wearing feathered wings, breaking his neck in the resulting fall. Eight centuries later the poet, John Taylor, commented 'On high the tempests have much power to wrecke, then best to bide beneath and safest for the necke'.

JUST AS MANY PREDICTED, manned ascending flight would first be demonstrated through the application of lighter-than-air craft – but not until the late eighteenth century, as detailed later.

Returning briefly to the medieval world, it then seemed that artificial wings were the most likely means of achieving some measure of flying success, although neither science had produced much real evidence of viability. Bladud, the ninth king of Britain, died in about 843 BC after attempting to fly from the Temple of Apollo in Trinavantum (London) using feather-covered wings. Oliver of Malmesbury, the Benedictine 'Flying Monk' whose actual name was Eilmer, broke his legs in about 1020 after leaping from Malmesbury Abbey, while Saracen of Constantinople was also an eleventh-century victim when his specially strengthened ribbed cloak suffered structural failure. The fact that Oliver had survived is generally believed to indicate that he had managed some limited gliding flight, and he put his lack of complete success down to the need for tail surfaces.

Many wonders of fourteenth-century China (then Cathay) came to light in Europe through the remarkable stories of Marco Polo, the Venetian merchant traveller. He told of man-carrying tethered kites, used to predict the likelihood of a good voyage for sailors by the success of the flight; whether this was an omen or a scientific means of gauging the strength of the wind is uncertain. Earlier, in 1306, China had been the setting for the first documented and successful quasi-parachute descents, made as part of the coronation celebrations for Emperor Fo-Kien; documentation found in Canton by a missionary in 1694 claimed also that a balloon ascent had been made at the same celebration, which, if true, rewrites the history of lighter-than-air flight.

LEONARDO DA VINCI'S CONTRIBUTION TO THE SCIENCE OF FLYING is a matter of conjecture. It may be suggested that it is because he so meticulously sketched and noted many designs and concepts that historians arguably accord to him more importance in aviation terms than he might actually deserve. In truth, most of his aeronautical studies were clearly unworkable, whilst some drew heavily on the concepts of others, as was quite normal within such circles at the time. For example, his square-section hand-held parachute of about 1485 is generally regarded as the first known design of its type. Yet, Fontana's description of a conical apparatus for flying experiments has similitude to da Vinci's subsequent 'pyramid' design – and

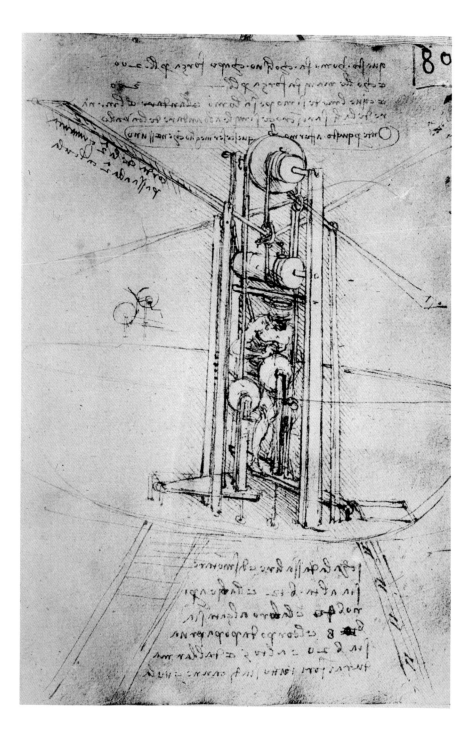

both men lived their lives in the same area of
Europe. A Venetian by the name of Fausto
Veranzio was the first to have a parachute design
published, in 1595, this time a square cloth
attached to a frame and with four shroud ropes
leading to a body harness.

Leonardo da Vinci was though, by any
standard, a genius of his time. As an artist,
sculptor and architect he was extraordinary, and
his research into the workings of the human body
was truly the effort of a genius, yet he is
remembered equally as a philosopher, engineer
and inventor. He appears to have been truly
fascinated by the idea of human flight, and yet
his legacy in this field is of far less value than his
art, his buildings and his remarkable human
physiological studies.

Born in 1452, his working life took him
through a frenzy of ideas that cascaded so freely
from his mind that he often left one project or
masterpiece unfinished while he began
something entirely new. Yet, strangely, it was to
be his thorough knowledge of anatomy, through
dissection and study, that would lead him to one
of his greatest errors of judgement: his belief that
a human had sufficient muscle power to achieve
ascending flight when aided by mechanical
apparatus, an error compounded by his
misunderstanding of how a bird flies through the
air. However ingenious his wing mechanisms
were for recreating what he perceived to be the
movement and functions of a bird's or bat's
flapping wing, his concepts were flawed from the
outset.

The word 'helicopter' is also attributed to da Vinci, taken from the Greek for spiral and wing (helix and
pteron). Without an understanding of aerofoils, da Vinci produced a 'corkscrew' design for vertical flight,
with the rotor constructed from starched flaxen linen over a steel wire frame and powered by the pilot
winding a rope around a central mast and pulling it to create spin. Again, such a concept was not new,
as small 'pull-string' toy helicopters had been in existence since the fourteenth century, one having been

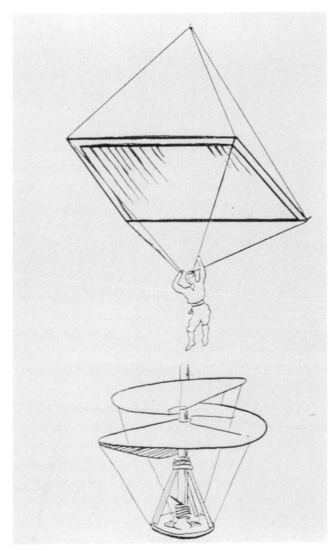

above

Da Vinci's hand-held, square-section parachute of *c.* 1485 is often described as the first design for a proper parachute. Yet Fontana earlier described a conical apparatus for use in hot-air experiments which possessed most of the attributes of da Vinci's parachute. Below this is da Vinci's spiral wing or corkscrew helicopter – no more practical than his ornithopters – to be driven by a spinning mast.

illustrated in a Flemish manuscript of 1325. In da Vinci's case, his full-size helicopter could never have worked.

It is unknown whether he built any of his many flying designs for trial, and in retrospect this can be judged as a misfortune. Those who believe he did, usually cite as evidence the existence of sketches and notes that detail the necessary pre-testing procedures. Conversely, given that he was an habitual note-taker, as no records exist of the results of testing, others conclude that he did not. However, a great many of his papers were lost or destroyed after his death. In truth, there is the distinct possibility that some scale models could have been tested, and perhaps even some full-scale ornithopters and other types under very controlled conditions, such as inside tall buildings, but their failure to fly may have curtailed his wish to record them further. Either way, a sustained programme of actual experimentation never happened, with unfortunate results: for example, his most promising glider design had no tail, yet a separate design featured tail surfaces. Actual experimentation might have brought these features together into one potentially successful design, but *theory* is no substitute for *practice* when attempting to perfect both design and suitable construction materials. It would be left to others to piece together the parts that would ultimately lead to success.

In recent years, attempts have been made to recreate some of da Vinci's machines, to prove him correct and way ahead of his time. Given the allowance that his drawings are sometimes hard to interpret, it should still be the plan in such endeavours to recreate faithfully all that is possible in order to test da Vinci's work properly. So often, however, replicas are modified to fit modern knowledge, which defeats the point: taking the wing, say, from one design and fitting it with features from another, not using da Vinci's sketched method of flight control but instead adopting a modern hang-glider system, and more, cannot provide a valid conclusion.

Modified replicas that differ in essential details, with adaptations to fit modern knowledge of aeronautics, have also been used to try to prove the claims of other aviation pioneers. In da Vinci's case, his legacy to many sciences is such that it makes no difference whatsoever that his flying studies were not entirely correct, and will never affect his standing as a man of pure genius.

THE RENAISSANCE PERIOD OF THE FOURTEENTH TO SIXTEENTH CENTURIES might have witnessed a revival in literature and art, but, as in da Vinci's case, it added little to a real understanding of aeronautics. Even de Lana-Terzi in the seventeenth century hardly extended aviation learning, but history does record stories of actual flying using apparatus that can at best be termed 'basic'. Whether true or not, the

seventeenth-century flight of the Turk, Hezarfen Celebi, who is said to have made a gliding flight from a tower at Galata and landed without injury in the centre of nearby Scutari, is well known to historians, although difficult to accept at face value. Yet, strangely, because of contemporary reports, there appears even less doubt about some other 'flights' which seem far more fanciful.

In 1678 a French locksmith named Besnier was reported to have made several flights in Sablé after jumping from a roof and tower. What underlies interest in these flights is that Besnier's flying apparatus was so primitive. Contemporary illustrations suggest that he held a pole over each shoulder, at the ends of which were attached hinged surfaces that would fold during the upwards movement and spread during the downwards, as a form of ornithopter. Using his shoulders as pivot points, his hands and the ropes attached to his ankles provided the up-and-down momentum. For such a basic device, it seems hard to imagine that Besnier could have flown at all, but there appears little doubt that he at least managed something that resembled a survivable glide, and he even sold a set of 'wings' to another would-be aeronaut from Guibre, who also achieved flight.

Although wing-flapping ornithopters continued to attract designers even into the early twentieth century, the technology had nowhere to go, despite the eventual application of engines to replace human power. Yet, it must be recorded that a small powered model aeroplane, built in 1647 by the Italian, Titus Livio Burattini, who then lived at the court of King Wladyslaw IV of Poland, flew with two sets of flapping wings that used springs and two sets of fixed wings, in tandem. What is more, some of the greatest pioneers of gliding flight in the nineteenth century, who anticipated moving on to powered flying machines, still viewed 'flappers' as having aeronautical potential when coupled to lightweight engines; these included the greatest of them all, the famed Otto Lilienthal. But, first, the eighteenth century would be the setting for man's first ascent skywards, with de Gusmão having provided the kick-start.

Simplicity Can Be Best

MANNED FLIGHT, IN THE PROPER SENSE, WAS FINALLY REALISED IN THE EIGHTEENTH CENTURY, when the first practical ascending craft finally appeared, and it was de Gusmão's model balloon of 1709 that had pointed the way. The dream of sustained heavier-than-air flight had to wait for future generations, while the more simple technology of lighter-than-air took centre stage.

One of the great misconceptions surrounding the history of ballooning is that hot-air balloons came about because there was no alternative 'lifting' element. Not true. In 1766 the English chemist, Henry Cavendish, isolated 'inflammable air' or Phlogiston gas, later named hydrogen by Lavoisier. In 1781 the Italian, Tiberius Cavallo, used gas-filled soap bubbles to demonstrate the lifting properties of hydrogen, but his attempts to fly bladders containing the same gas failed, having taken too little account of their weight. Yet, only a little time after, on 27 August 1783, a 3.5 m-diameter hydrogen balloon made from silk coated with gum and capable of lifting a 9-kg load was launched from the Champ-des-Mars in Paris by 37-year-old Professor Jacques Alexandre César Charles. It drifted for 45 minutes before coming to rest at Gonesse, where it was destroyed by frenzied peasants who believed it to be supernatural. Whilst not the first-ever flight by a large unmanned balloon *per se*, it was the first by a hydrogen balloon and came about only weeks after the famed Montgolfier brothers had first publicly demonstrated an 11-m unmanned hot-air balloon at Annonay. Before the end of that year, on 1 December, Charles and a companion made a manned, free flight in a much larger hydrogen balloon, watched by a crowd of 400,000, flying 43 km from Paris to Nesles.

It is a remarkable quirk of history that Jacques Charles did not become a household name for future generations world-wide, whereas the Montgolfier brothers did. With his flight of 1 December 1783, Charles virtually killed off at a stroke the long-term future for first-generation hot-air balloons, and this only six weeks after the Montgolfier brothers had been responsible for the first properly recorded and witnessed manned balloon flight in the history of mankind.

The story of the French Montgolfier brothers' historic achievement, albeit soon to be eclipsed, began at Avignon in 1779 when Joseph Montgolfier built a tiny 2 m-diameter parachute and tested it – using a sheep – with some success. At Vidalon-les-Annonay, where his father owned a paper mill, he continued his experiments using a larger parachute that was capable of sustaining his own weight. As time would show, this was one of the few occasions in which he became personally involved as a 'test pilot' in his own flying experiments.

One fateful day at his lodgings in Avignon, Joseph pondered over the embers from his fire rising up the chimney. When later he noticed that his shirt, drying close to the fire, filled out, he made the connection between the

The Ascent of the Aerial Balloon.

heat generated by the fire and its 'lifting' properties being 'captured' within the material. In November 1782 he made a taffeta bag and held it close to a fire. As he thought, once filled with warm air, it drifted up to the ceiling. An idea struck home.

With his brother, Jacques-Etienne, Joseph now put in hand a series of secret experiments for 'aerostatic machines', as he called them, each paper envelope becoming steadily larger. Finally, at Annonay on 25 April 1783, the brothers secretly released a paper balloon of 12 m diameter, inflated by the heat from burning materials and capable of lifting an estimated 200-kg load. It was a huge success, rising to an altitude of 300 m.

It was time to go public, and on 4 June that same year in the market place at Annonay they inflated a new balloon of linen and paper which, to the delight of the vast gathering of onlookers, rose to about

below

De Rozier and the Marquis d'Arlandes rise during the first-ever untethered, manned balloon flight, on 21 November 1783, attaining an altitude of about 900 m. The ropes attached to the two tall poles, used for earlier tethered flights, are no longer needed and are twisted around the poles to keep them clear of the main event (see page 27).

1,800 m. But things were about to go wrong for the brothers in an unexpected way, at the very time they were heading for even greater aeronautical achievement.

The success of their latest balloon encouraged the brothers to contact the Académie des Sciences in Paris, an organisation that became greatly enthused with the idea of balloon research and asked for a further demonstration. While a new and highly decorated balloon was being prepared, and the fame of the Montgolfiers was spreading internationally, the Académie set about raising public funding for balloon research. Whether a far-sighted gesture, or a stab in the back, much of the money raised did not go to the Montgolfiers, however, but was given instead to Jacques Charles for hydrogen balloon experimentation, including the purchase of iron filings and sulphuric acid to produce the gas itself. The resulting 3.5-m hydrogen balloon has already been described.

Although the Académie clearly favoured Charles's hydrogen balloon experiments, it was mindful of the contribution to flying made by the Montgolfiers and duly awarded the brothers sums of cash in August 1783. Other honours came their way, including further cash and a pension from King Louis XVI.

By September 1783 the Montgolfier Académie balloon was ready to show Académie members, the King, Queen Marie Antoinette and others, but rain destroyed the envelope and a new one had to be constructed in four days. To the delight of the huge crowds of onlookers, on 19 September the new 13 m-diameter envelope was inflated, and it rose from the ground, carrying below it a wicker cage containing a sheep, a cock and a duck, all of which survived the eight-minute flight to the Forest of Vaucresson.

It was now time for a manned flight, and with confidence the Montgolfiers constructed a new 15 m-diameter hot-air balloon. Such an adventure clearly had its dangers and the King suggested that two criminals

right
On 7 January 1785
Frenchman Jean-Pierre
Blanchard and American
Dr John Jeffries flew the
English Channel in a
hydrogen balloon. The
following June de Rozier
and Jules Romain
attempted the same
journey, but in the
opposite direction, in a
composite hot-air and
hydrogen balloon. They
are depicted here
leaving Boulogne. The
combination of fire and
gas was ill-conceived
and both men were
killed when vented gas
was ignited. These were
the first deaths in a
ballooning accident.

under death sentence should be used as expendable guinea-pigs. But the very idea that such men should become the world's first aeronauts, and go into the history books for posterity, was too much for Jean Francois Pilâtre de Rozier, who offered himself for the risky venture. And so, on 15 October 1783, de Rozier mounted the gallery around the base of the balloon and, while it was tethered by rope to the ground, he allowed the balloon to rise and fall a few times at low level before giving the command to let it go up to the full length of the restraining ropes, about 26 m. By using holes provided in the neck of the envelope to throw additional straw and wool on to the brazier, de Rozier managed to stay aloft for over four minutes. At last, a human had flown in ascending flight! Over the coming days he made further tethered ascents.

Now joined by the Marquis d'Arlandes, on 21 November 1783 de Rozier gave the order to let go and together they rose from the Château La Muette in the Bois de Boulogne to make the world's first free (untethered), manned flight in a balloon, during which they drifted over Paris and landed 25 minutes later on the Butte-aux-Cailles.

Within months balloon ascents had also taken place in several other countries, mostly using Montgolfier types, but the writing was already on the wall for hot-air ballooning: in September 1784 a great aerial voyage was made over Britain by the Italian, Vincenzo Lunardi of Lucca, flying a hydrogen balloon from London to Hertfordshire. By 1789 the Montgolfier balloon business had virtually collapsed.

Montgolfier-type balloons had set the standard and, in the event, had demonstrated their ability to fly for very respectable periods of time, but they lacked the development potential and ultimately the flying duration of the hydrogen usurpers. Only with the reinvention of hot-air ballooning for pleasure in the latter part of the twentieth century, using new high-tech fabrics and gas burners, did this branch of aeronautics make any further contribution to aviation. Yet, for a short time, it was cutting-edge technology and utterly awe-inspiring.

THE SO-CALLED FATHER OF AERIAL NAVIGATION WAS AN ENGLISHMAN, SIR GEORGE CAYLEY. Born in Brompton, Yorkshire, in December 1773, he was a true aristocrat with the same combined qualities of a theologian and practical inventor that could be found in many men of his day who industrialised the world.

Although he was to champion aeronautical and cause heavier-than-air flying to be established, to say that he began modestly is, without question, an understatement. In 1796 he produced a tiny model helicopter powered by the bowdrill method and comprising merely a central stick and 'rotors' made from feathers pushed into corks at each end of the stick. As the string of the bowdrill unwound, the two rotors contra-rotated. In all essentials it was similar to the model produced by Launoy and Bienvenu in France in 1784, although they had adopted two-blade rotors, as opposed to Cayley's four-blade types.

After the model helicopter, Cayley began original research into several different aspects of flight, his most important contribution being the identification of the mathematical principles behind lift, thrust and drag. He cast aside the idea that human muscles could produce sufficient power for flight, and championed the concept that a flying machine had to be realistically proportioned.

In 1804, using a whirling arm rig fitted with interchangeable surfaces, he conducted experiments connected with aerodynamics, lift and wing loading, concluding that a concave surface was more efficient for producing lift than a flat surface, even when the flat surface was angled from the horizontal. He also realised that wing dihedral helped lateral stability, and that the tail of an aircraft should comprise not only a rudder but surfaces capable of 'up and down' movement. To test his ideas, in 1804 Cayley produced a model glider with a simple kite-type wing set at a high angle of incidence, a stick fuselage and adjustable cruciform tail unit. This was the first-ever aeroplane (albeit a model) of classic aeroplane layout.

By 1809 Cayley had detailed all the necessary attributes for a workable aeroplane; he had also envisaged the use of a gas or internal combustion engine to provide power, believing steam engines to be too heavy. In the following year he put forward the argument for braced biplane and triplane wings, and of streamlining airframes.

To further his researches, in 1809 Cayley constructed a large glider capable of being flown with or

above

A modern reproduction of Cayley's man-carrying Governable Parachute glider, the design of which had been published in *Mechanics' Magazine* in September 1852. The original glider had carried Cayley's coachman into the air in 1853, prompting the servant's wish to hand in his notice of employment.

without a pilot, which flew beautifully for long distances when released from a hilltop (unmanned). It had been his intention to use this full-size glider for powered experiments, but unfortunately it was destroyed in an accident that same year; although he had little time for ornithopters, had he fitted an engine to the 1809 craft it is generally believed that it would have driven either an 'oblique flyer' – a propeller – or designated flapping areas of the main wings.

Then, in 1849, eight years before his death, Cayley took the world one step closer to its dream. Having constructed a tailed triplane with a wing area some ten per cent greater than that of his 1809 glider, but of overall lighter weight, a ten-year-old boy was put on board and the aircraft was towed down a hill against a slight breeze, carrying the boy aloft. In June 1853 a similar experiment with his coachman led to a flight of several hundred metres, ending in a capsize and the famous words, 'Please, Sir George, I wish to give my notice. I was hired to drive, not to fly.'

Cayley was never single-minded, however, and had realised early in his investigations that the immediate future for air travel rested firmly with lighter-than-air craft. In 1816 he had envisaged steerable airships with wings or propellers, using steam engines for motive power, and theorised on the construction of rigid airships with wooden frames or metal envelopes containing separate gas bags. In 1843, he had also produced the design for a convertiplane, using four separate eight-blade rotors for vertical lift, the blades of which could be closed together to form circular wing surfaces for horizontal flight after twin propellers on shafts had been started.

AT THE FIRST MEETING OF THE NEWLY FOUNDED AERONAUTICAL SOCIETY OF GREAT BRITAIN, on 27 June 1866, marine engineer Francis Herbert Wenham delivered his historic paper 'Aerial Locomotion', which he had written in 1859. Wenham believed in Cayley's ideas on cambered wings but also advocated that the wing should have a thicker section at its leading edge. He thought that, as most of the lift was derived from the front portion of the wing, a long and narrow wing would be the most efficient, but that this needed to be divided into a multiplane structure to allow a manageable span. As a result of his researches, Wenham is recognised as having been the first person to deduce correctly the main properties of a cambered aerofoil (for example, lift distribution).

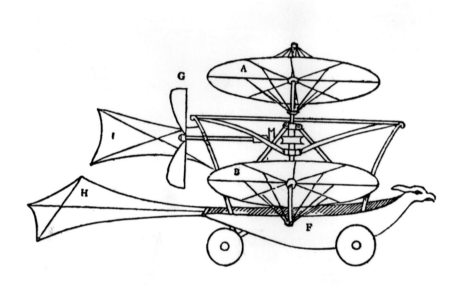

Shortly before he delivered his lecture, Wenham tried tentatively to reinforce his theory by testing a 4.87 m-span glider configured to use five or six wings in the form of a collapsible multicellular box-kite, using thin holland (linen) material as the covering that took aerodynamic form when the horizontal surfaces were distended by the wind. This appears to have been the first such structure in history (discounting the dragon head box-kite structures of some medieval kites). The glider had no tail, and the pilot lay prone on a board beneath the wings, using his feet to operate 'flappers' at the ends of long lever arms extending beyond the wingtips; the flappers might be viewed as closely related to an early concept considered by Cayley, as an alternative to propellers. Wenham attempted to become airborne after running into the wind, but the glider proved far too flimsy and so he constructed another incorporating considerable stiffening. This glider was consequently much heavier; no records of the trials are known to exist. Nonetheless, through the later work of Hargrave and Chanute, both of whom became familiar with Wenham's work, the box-kite structure was developed further. Wenham is also remembered for constructing the first wind tunnel with John Browning in 1871, used by the Aeronautical Society.

THE BOX-KITE CONFIGURATION for aeroplane wings appears at first glance to be a simple development and of little importance, but this perception would be incorrect. It actually had a profound effect on early powered flying in Europe.

above
Sir George Cayley's 1843 convertiplane, intended to combine the flying qualities of a helicopter and aeroplane. The project was detailed in *Mechanics' Magazine* at that time, and it has been said that Cayley found inspiration from the thoughts of Henson.

above

Lawrence Hargrave and his helper, Swaine, during experiments with cellular kites. Hargrave's greatest contribution to aviation was to take the known advantages of superimposed wings and add vertical stabilising surfaces between, leading to the development of braced box-kite wings for aircraft, as adopted by others for actual flying machines. Hargrave's box-kite structure was also used on meteorological kites.

English-born Lawrence Hargrave, living in Australia, began to study aviation in 1882, and by 1884 he had experimented with no fewer than 50 rubber-driven models. He favoured propulsion by 'flappers' that imitated the action of a bird's primary feathers. In 1889 he also built a three-cylinder rotary engine driven by compressed air, the first rotary engine for aeronautical use. However, his preoccupation with stability essential for free-flying models – and, later, his kites – distracted him to the need for a pilot-operated control system.

In January 1891 Hargrave sketched an idea for a basic hang-glider, with a man hanging at arm's length beneath a flat monoplane surface. Soon he began to appreciate the advantage of curved surfaces, and tested various models with tandem monoplane wings, and then, in 1893, with multiple surfaces. That same year, inspired by Wenham's work, he began testing cellular kites, and during the ensuing year developed this into the braced box-kite, probably his most significant contribution to aviation.

Inspired by Lilienthal's gliding flights, Hargrave went on to build a tandem monoplane with its wings at an acute dihedral angle. Two attempts to fly the glider in June 1894 had little success and he abandoned it, devoting his time thereafter to the design of man-carrying box-kites, but these were not constructed. Interestingly, though, American-born Samuel Franklin Cody used the multicellular approach to develop man-lifting kites in Farnborough, England, from 1899, leading to the development of manned observation kites, used in the Great War of 1914–18.

A TRINITY OF PIONEERS now took the science of gliding to such advancement that it became inevitable that someone would, in the not-too-distant future, make that last step to a successful powered aeroplane. For a time it appeared that it could even be one of the three pioneers themselves, indeed, the greatest of them all, German engineer Otto Lilienthal.

After demobilisation from the army in 1871, Lilienthal resumed the aviation experiments he had begun earlier. His principal interest was the ornithopter, but he decided that the only way to gain a proper insight into flight was initially to test fixed-wing hang-gliders, with the ultimate aim of devising a machine with engine-driven flappers at its wingtips.

Lilienthal's first two fixed-wing gliders, bird-like monoplanes, built in 1889 and 1890, were mainly for ground trials and were unsuccessful. He followed these with his partially successful 1891 model, tested at Derwitz. This third glider featured heavily cambered wings, which were subsequently reduced in span from 7.6 m to 5.5 m. A rigid fin was added for the first time. Another glider was tested at Südende in 1892, this time a curvaceous monoplane with a 9.5-m span. As with all his gliders, control in pitch, roll and yaw was achieved by the pilot swinging his body and legs to shift the position of the centre of gravity.

The following year Lilienthal erected a flat-roofed hangar on a height called the Maihöhe at Steglitz, a position from which he could launch himself from 10 m above the ground. Here he tested his first glider to have folding wings to aid transportation. Spanning 7 m, it featured a tailplane with upwards movement to prevent a nose-dive should the glider be stopped in the air by a sudden gust; this device became standard on all his later gliders and many reasonably successful flights were achieved.

Also in 1893 Lilienthal constructed a powered ornithopter of 6.85-m span, with six flapping wingtip blades on each side, powered by a small 2-hp carbonic acid gas motor. Although this machine was tested as a glider both with and without its engine installed, no powered flights were attempted.

In 1894 three new gliders were built, while he also had a 15-m artificial hill raised at Lichterfelde, incorporating a hangar, to permit take-offs in any direction according to the wind. The first of the new gliders was the *Model Stölln*, named after a town in the Rhinower Hills, where Lilienthal was now flying regularly. A hoop of willow ahead of the pilot was intended to absorb the shock from a rough

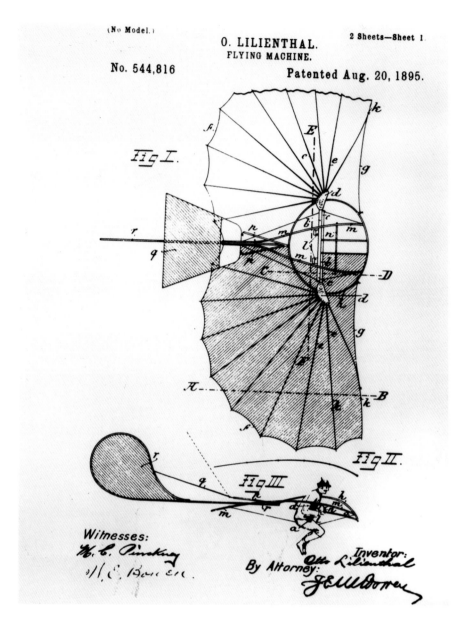

Fig I.

Fig II.

Fig III.

Witnesses:

Inventor:
Otto Lilienthal

By Attorney:

landing and, indeed, Lilienthal did crash several times when the glider stalled and nose-dived from considerable heights above the ground, allowing him to escape with minor injuries. The second new glider was the *Sturmflügelmodell*, suited to flying in stronger winds due to its reduced wing area. The third was the *Normal-Segelapparat* – simply his standard sailing machine – which proved to be the most reliable. This had a span of 6.7 m and a tailplane level with the fin, instead of ahead of it. In this glider Lilienthal made controlled flights of up to 250 m, and he built eight replicas for sale or to give to other pioneers.

Lilienthal's *Vorflügelapparat* of 1895 had leading-edge flaps along its 8.8-m span, hinging downwards to help prevent nose-dives. It also featured wingtip fins operated by the movement of his body, but these were quickly abandoned. This was followed by two biplanes, as he then believed that shorter-span wings could be better controlled. Trials showed that his assumption was correct, and he flew these safely in winds of over 38 km/h, and even demonstrated a hover in flight, when he could talk to onlookers.

opposite

Lilienthal built his first biplane glider in 1895, as No 13, followed by No 14 with reduced wing area in the same year. His third and last biplane was No 15, produced in 1895–96 and identified by having a smaller upper wing. This photograph, taken in 1896, shows the grace of these peeled willow wand and waxed cotton material gliders.

above

Otto Lilienthal protected his advanced design for hang gliders by obtaining patents. Despite this Lilienthal was always prepared to give advice and share knowledge, one beneficiary being Pilcher in Great Britain.

Lilienthal's prolific output of craft was planned to continue during 1895–96, now partly aimed at exploring powered flying. While continuing to fly his existing trusted gliders, a new machine was begun featuring six flapping blades at the ends of its 8.5 m-span wing, powered by a new carbonic acid gas motor. Another planned newcomer was the *Gelenkflügelapparat*, a monoplane with thick-section, double-surface wings with two jointed spars. However, Lilienthal's pioneering efforts were about to end. Tragically, on 9 August 1896, while flying a standard monoplane, he was gusted to a halt and the glider stalled and then sideslipped to the ground. Lilienthal's spine was broken and he died the following day.

In just six years Lilienthal had progressed flying immeasurably and had taken the science to the very edge of its powered era. In doing so he had accomplished some 2,500 flights with his willow and cotton material gliders. In his final year of experimentation he had also conceived wing warping as a method of flight control, as later used by the Wright brothers and others. Where da Vinci dreamed, Lilienthal flew centuries later, a place where no man had been before.

above

Britain's leading gliding pioneer was Lilienthal disciple Percy Pilcher, here seen with his large and heavy *Beetle*. Testing proved a disappointment, with too little control, resulting in the reconstruction of his first glider, the *Bat*.

A DISCIPLE OF LILIENTHAL was British-born Percy Sinclair Pilcher who, in early 1895, in Glasgow, began building his first glider named *Bat*. In most respects it was similar to Lilienthal's craft, although with more complex bracing. Originally without a tailplane, it flew badly in tests that June. Having already been advised to fit a horizontal tail by Lilienthal during a visit to Germany in April, he subsequently modified the *Bat* and the improvements were obvious. However, having found that the glider's high stability prevented proper control, he set about building a new, larger and modified glider which became the *Beetle*. Unfortunately, this was too heavy and gave Pilcher too little control, so he reconstructed his first glider, reducing wing dihedral. The results were encouraging.

Having built two more gliders for testing in 1896, the *Gull* and the *Hawk*, both meant to have small engines fitted once they had been successfully flown as gliders, he relocated to Kent. There he became an assistant to Sir Hiram Maxim who, on 31 July 1894, had seen his own vast 372-sq-m and impractical steam-driven aeroplane lift briefly from the ground during a test run. Pilcher's association with Maxim lasted only until 1897, however, but Pilcher had already designed a 4-hp petrol engine for the *Hawk* and thereafter established an engineering concern to develop it.

Still in 1896, Pilcher received a letter from the American, Octave Chanute, who had developed a classic biplane hang-glider that was outstanding in its performance when flown by Augustus Moore Herring (Chanute being too old to fly), having originally begun his own experimentation by improving Lilienthal-type designs. As a result, Pilcher designed a quadruplane which could take the petrol engine when ready to be fitted, but then modified it into a triplane. At the end of September 1899 Pilcher arranged to demonstrate his new triplane but, while first attempting to fly *Hawk* during a day of poor weather, the glider collapsed and Pilcher was fatally injured.

below

Pilcher with his most successful glider, the 1896 *Hawk*, with fixed wheels to help manoeuvre it while on the ground. *Hawk* was intended for conversion into a powered machine once testing had been completed and the engine fully developed, but in 1899 it crashed and Pilcher lost his life.

right
After experimenting with multi-winged gliders, American Octave Chanute developed the 'classic' superimposed braced biplane layout, here fitted with a box-kite type tail unit. Too old to fly his own craft, Chanute enlisted the help of Herring and Avery.

SEVERAL AMERICAN EXPERIMENTERS WERE INSPIRED BY LILIENTHAL, his work receiving a great deal of publicity through the efforts of Chanute, a railway engineer who kept abreast of aviation developments world-wide. Chanute's book of 1894, *Progress in Flying Machines*, was the first comprehensive history of heavier-than-air flying and is known to have inspired the Wright brothers in their aeronautical interests.

Lilienthal's greatest disciple in America was, however, Augustus Herring who, between 1894 and 1895, built three monoplane gliders based on the German's designs, but these had only limited success. Herring then showed interest in Chanute's multiplane concept with automatic stability device, and began tests using scale models. Soon the two Americans collaborated on a full-size glider, which was initially tested with no fewer than 12 wings of 1.8-m span each (eight in front and four at the rear), but the configuration went through several changes during short-duration tests in 1896.

A new Chanute glider followed, originally a triplane of 4.87-m span and weighing as little as 14 kg,

above

Augustus Moore Herring about to launch himself from the dunes around the shore of Lake Michigan in June 1896, where Octave Chanute had established his main proving ground. The biplane glider has a cruciform tail unit

but later converted into the classic biplane when Herring found it possessed too much lift. A secret of the design was its rigid bracing with wires, using the Pratt truss system used on bridges. On 11 September 1896, Herring achieved a 77-m glide lasting 14 seconds. It was an outstanding success, and it is a matter of history that the Wright brothers became close friends of Chanute, learning much from his braced biplane structure and selecting a similar layout for their own aircraft.

The groundwork for the future development of practical powered flying machines had been completed, and it was now to be a race to glory!

Hidden Pioneers

previous spread
Wilbur Wright flying a
Model A at Pau, France, in
1908, the same year he
taught Frenchman Paul
Tissandier to fly. On
20 May 1909 Tissandier
established the first FAI-
approved world speed
record for powered
airplanes, at 54.77 km/h,
flying a Wright at Pau.

below
Artist's impression of the
full-size Henson *Aerial
Steam Carriage*, which
was to have a wing-span
of 45.72 m, weigh about
1,360 kg, and be powered
by a 30 horsepower
steam engine ordered
from John Stringfellow.

IT IS A MATTER OF PRIDE that various countries independently celebrate having been the birthplace of manned and powered flight. The former USSR claimed that honour for Alexander Mozhaiskii, France points to Félix du Temple de la Croix and Clément Ader, and the USA proclaim the Wright brothers, while also in the running could be New Zealand's Richard William Pearse, Austria's Wilhelm Kress, Germany's Carl Jatho, and so the list goes on. But who, actually, was first?

In a curious way, all could be. To explain why, history must return to 1844–47. Then, Englishman William Samuel Henson conducted trials with a 6.1-m wing span scale model of his proposed *Aerial Steam Carriage*, the full-size version of which was anticipated to become the first-ever commercial airliner for world-wide service with the projected Aerial Transit Company. The full-size *Aerial Steam Carriage* was to be a curious mix of fanciful Victoriana and high technology, with double-skinned cambered wings,

full vertical and horizontal tail surfaces, an enclosed fuselage for the crew and passengers, a tricycle
undercarriage and engine-driven propellers. Unfortunately, even when aided by a launching ramp during
trials at Chard in Somerset, England, the model hardly flew and the whole project was abandoned. The
model was, however, the first to use a steam engine.

Henson's colleague in the construction of the model *Aerial Steam Carriage* had been John Stringfellow,
who had already begun working on his own less-elaborate steam-powered model by 1846. In 1848, the
year Henson emigrated to the USA, Stringfellow began trials with this 3.2 m-span model at Chard. The
entire craft weighed only 3.6 kg, or 3.8 kg with fuel and water. For launching, it was attached to a bogie
that ran along a cable on the inside of a 24 m-long building, with automatic release. Although damaged
after stalling on its first release, Stringfellow's model was repaired and the angle of the tail reduced. This
time, after release, it gradually rose in flight until 'captured' in a hanging cloth at the far end of the building.

Other similar flights followed. Then, once experiments moved to the Cremorne Gardens in London,
the model demonstrated a flight of 40 m. These are claimed to be the first successful flights by a powered
model aeroplane. However, seeing no means of reproducing his success with a full-size version,
Stringfellow gave up his experiments for many years.

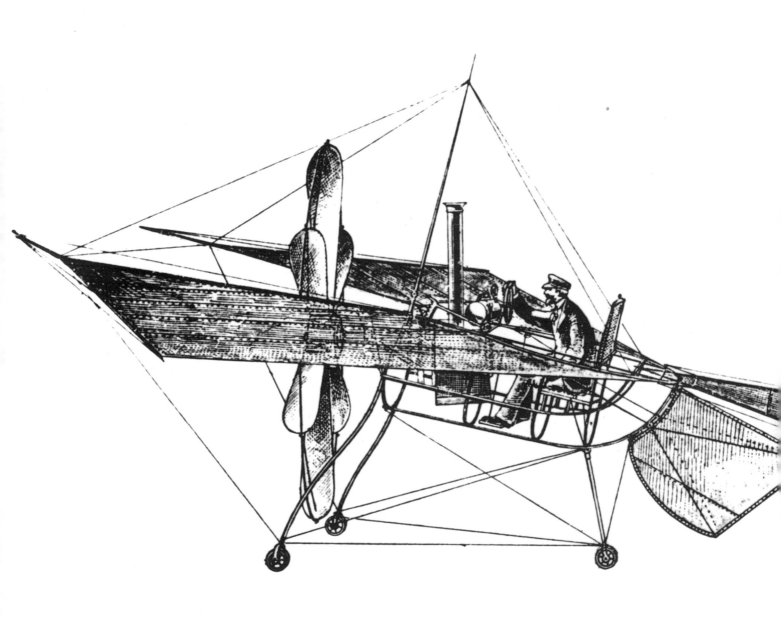

left
Félix du Temple de la Croix was
awarded the first French patent
for a complete aeroplane design,
on 2 May 1857. Following tests
with a tiny model, he spent nearly
two decades building and
modifying a full-size aeroplane,
which 'hopped' in 1874.

below
Stringfellow's
aeronautical steam
engine.

At the Crystal Palace, in 1868, The Aeronautical Society of Great Britain staged the world's first aeronautical exhibition, for which Stringfellow built and exhibited a fine steam-powered model triplane and a light aeronautical steam engine. Interestingly, the 1868 prize-winning engine eventually ended up at the Air and Space Museum in Washington, USA, having been bought by Samuel Pierpont Langley.

Although witnessed, the achievements of Stringfellow's monoplane are often challenged for the accolade of being the first successful flights by a powered model aeroplane, partly because of the method of launch and partly due to the duration of flight achieved. The main challenger came from France.

In May 1857, Félix du Temple de la Croix was

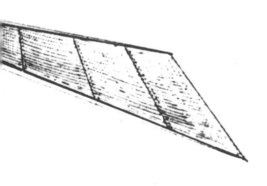

given the first French patent for a complete aeroplane design. At that time du Temple constructed a tiny model aeroplane, weighing just 0.7 kg. With a boat-like hull, monoplane wings set at 14° to the horizontal, a wheeled undercarriage, and fitted successively with a clockwork and then a small steam engine, it flew during tests in 1857–58, coming to land safely after its propeller stopped by floating down on its wings. This little aeroplane was, therefore, the first powered model to take off from the ground under its own power, albeit using a ramp at launch.

So, the first model to make a successful flight could be said to have been Henson's, or Stringfellow's, or du Temple's, depending upon whether the duration of a flight or the method of launch are deemed important. Or perhaps it was Titus Livio Burattini's powered ornithopter of 1647, mentioned earlier. Disregarding the ornithopter for almost certainly having been hand-launched and of very limited ability, there is no doubt that Henson's model aeroplane actually flew first, but the flight did not last any length of time and so was not 'sustained'. And, like du Temple's monoplane which probably flew the best of all the models, it had used a ramp to assist take-off. Stringfellow's monoplane preceded du Temple's and managed a reasonable distance, and rose in flight, but was effectively air launched. Therefore, from an historical viewpoint, the 'first' accolade is probably best shared amongst all the contenders, although most historians favour du Temple.

Of many other aeronautical modellers who followed, perhaps Alphonse Pénaud should be mentioned, as he invented the twisted rubber band method of powering models, initially used on a tiny and primitive Launoy and Bienvenu-type helicopter in 1870 and later on his *planophore* model aeroplane that managed flights of up to 60 m from 1871. His plans to construct a full-size amphibious monoplane powered by a hydrocarbon engine came to nothing, although he patented the design with Paul Gauchot in 1876. This is memorable for being an entirely practical project for its time, incorporating cambered wing ribs with semi-structural wooden or metal skins on the top and bottom, streamlined bracing wires, variable-pitch

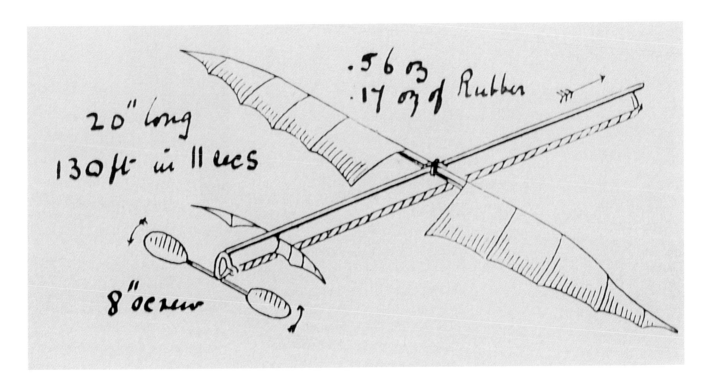

20" long
130 ft in 11 secs

.56 oz
.17 oz of Rubber

8" screw

above

Alphonse Pénaud's *planophore* twisted rubber-powered aeroplane model of 1871, which followed earlier 'flights' in 1870 of a simple rubber-powered helicopter model. The *planophore*, which could have either a pusher or tractor propeller, proved capable of flights of 60 m and allowed the study of longitudinal stability. To prevent the airframe rotating as the rubber unwound, a wing and tail surface on one side was twisted or a counter weight was added to the other.

tractor propellers (4-blade), a folding undercarriage with shock-absorbers, control of the elevators and rudder via a single handlebar with spring loading, and a range of flight instruments.

IT IS THE CONFUSION CAUSED BY THE TERMINOLOGY OF WHAT CONSTITUTES 'A FLIGHT' that also muddles the history of manned and powered aeroplanes. Certainly, if to achieve a recognised flight a full-size aeroplane had to be piloted, powered, controllable, self-launching from level ground, free-flying and capable of a reasonable duration in the air, then the Wright brothers were first. But is it correct to add so many conditions, or have they been used to distort history?

Félix du Temple de la Croix went on to construct a full-size craft, which underwent continual change over two decades. Beginning with 17 m-span wings, each using only two crossing hollow wooden spars, and ending with 30-m wings using riveted aluminium spars, the gummed fabric covering of each wing was allowed to billow out 'like the sails of a windmill'. Initially, power came from a hot-air motor driving a 4-m diameter tractor propeller with 12 wooden blades, but he subsequently changed this for a steam engine with lightweight boiler and condenser of his own design.

It appears that du Temple did not conduct a particularly vigorous test programme, although at Brest, in 1874, a young sailor was carried aloft on a short 'hop' flight after a ramp-assisted take-off. In this feat, he was first! In the following year, an Englishman by the name of Thomas Moy saw his unpiloted tandem-wing steam aeroplane, *Aerial Steamer*, lift a few centimetres from the ground while tethered to fly around a circular track. The significance was that the aeroplane lifted from level ground, without ramp assistance.

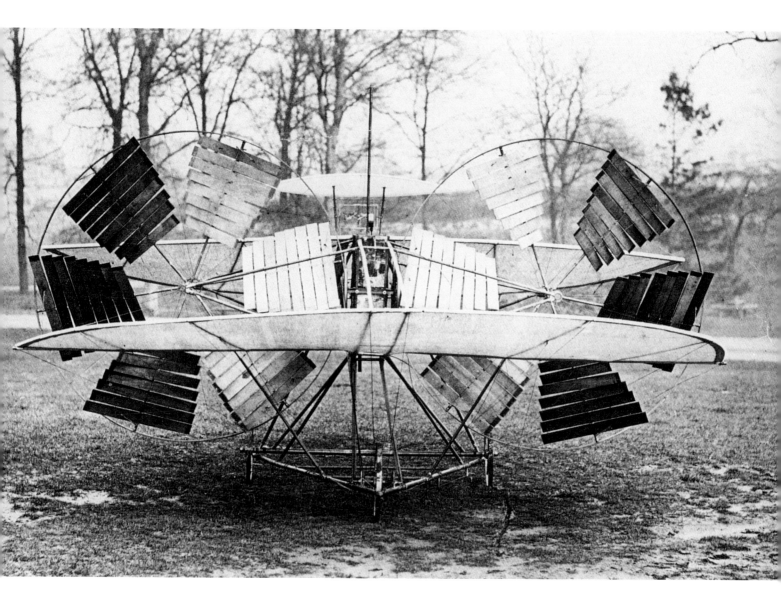

above

Thomas Moy's unpiloted tandem-wing *Aerial Steamer*, which just lifted off level ground in 1875 at the Crystal Palace in London. Each of the two propellers comprised six blades, each in turn made from eight small slats.

In Russia, Alexander Fedorovich Mozhaiskii, a captain in the Imperial Russian Navy, was granted a patent in 1881 for a full-size aeroplane displaying Henson influence. Earlier, Mozhaiskii had developed an interest in birdflight and kites, being towed aloft on a monoplane kite behind a three-horse troika. In 1876 he then turned to clockwork models and twisted rubber, and in 1881 began planning a full-size monoplane with a 22.5-m wing. This was to use three 4 m-diameter propellers, with one in the nose driven by a ten-hp steam engine and two mounted amidships surrounded by the low-aspect-ratio wing and belt-driven by a 20-hp steam engine carried in the boat-like fuselage. The engines were made in England, by Ahrbecker & Son, and Hamken of London. Although movable vertical and horizontal tail surfaces were provided, there was no provision for control in roll. The structure was supported on a four-wheel undercarriage.

Construction of Mozhaiskii's monoplane began in the summer of 1882, taking place on a plot on the military field at Krasnoye Selo, near St Petersburg, in all weathers and in the face of official indifference. An attempt at flight was made in 1884, with a mechanic on board, when the machine was apparently damaged. It has hitherto been claimed that a brief lift-off was made after launch down a ramp, but early records make no mention of a ramp, and it is now believed that the machine did not get off the ground at all, as it was seriously underpowered for its weight.

STEAM, WHICH HAD REVOLUTIONISED INDUSTRY AND PROVIDED THE MOTIVE POWER FOR RAILWAYS, continued to attract aeronautical interest in the late nineteenth century. Between 1882 and 1897, French inventor and engineer Clément Ader built and tested tailless monoplanes with deeply arched bat-form wings, influenced by nature. Although they were ingenious examples of the engineer's art in the Victorian era, they were over-ambitious and misguided creations that were to influence nobody.

Ader's first powered aeroplane, the *Éole* , completed in 1889, had a single propeller with four feather-like bamboo blades driven by a progressive 20-hp steam engine designed by Ader himself. Details of this machine were patented in April 1890, and on 9 October that year, in the grounds of the chateau of Madame Pereire near Gretz, Armainvilliers, Ader became airborne for 50 m at a height of 20 cm, witnessed by gardeners and Ader's employees. This far exceeded any achievement by du Temple, not least as it was supposedly from level ground, and may therefore be considered the first ever take-off by a powered man-carrying aeroplane. However, the machine had no elevator, no rudder and no true flight controls, and so was deemed to have insufficient stability. It is interesting to note, though, that Ader had provided himself with a hand-operated crank to adjust each wing to vary the centre of pressure, plus methods to vary each wing's area and camber, and a means of flexing the wings in the vertical plane without altering the angle of incidence. This huge workload meant that, in addition to the steam engine controls, Ader had expected to operate two pedals and six cranks with his feet and hands.

Although demonstrating many shortcomings, the *Éole* was still cutting-edge technology for the day, and so on 3 February 1892 the French Ministry of War commissioned an improved machine and awarded Ader a generous subsidy in excess of 650,000 francs.

Ader's next aeroplane, the *Avion II*, with a 30-hp steam engine, was abandoned before completion, but a new contract was agreed and a third machine, the *Avion III*, had been completed by the autumn of 1897. This resembled the *Éole*, but was powered by two of Ader's remarkable steam engines fed from a single boiler, with similar propellers as before; the propellers made use of a differential speed device.

above

It had been thought that the Russian Alexander Fedorovich Mozhaiskii had managed to see his steam-powered monoplane lift off the ground in 1884, piloted by a mechanic named Golubev. However, more recent evidence has cast doubt on previous claims. Underpowered for its weight, it would have required a downwards ramp or slope to gather speed and early records make no mention of these. Total wing and tail area of this large aeroplane was 372 sq m, and overall weight was 934 kg.

opposite top & bottom

Clement Ader's bat-like *Éole* managed to take off in October 1890 for a 50 m skim over level testing ground, with Ader himself at the controls. Ader noted that the aircraft was not sufficiently stable and that further studies were required to improve the apparatus.

Ader's military *Avion III* (shown here with wings folded) failed to take off during trials in October 1897. Although the official Commission advised the War Minister to back continued experiments, this view was rejected. Ader failed to find new backers and destroyed the *Éole*, his workshop and scientific/technical papers, but left the *Avion III* for preservation.

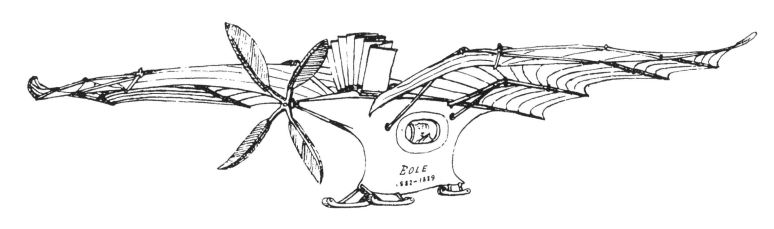

The simplified 16 m-span wings could be swung backwards or forwards together and this time Ader added a fabric-covered rudder operated by pedals which also controlled the rear undercarriage wheel. And, equally importantly for the Ministry, it was a two-seater capable of carrying a 75-kg bomb load.

Ader's first trial of the *Avion III* took place on a circular track at Satory on 12 October 1897. In the presence of officials, the aeroplane travelled along the ground for 1,400 m at low power, at a speed of 19–24 km/h, but it did not leave the ground, although the shallow wheel tracks indicated that the wings had carried much of the aircraft's weight. The second trial took place two days later. Although the rear wheel lifted, the aircraft remained stubbornly on the ground until it was struck by a gust of wind which lifted it off momentarily, slewing it over and leaving a wing, the propellers and wheels damaged. It was never tested again.

Nine years later, in 1906, Ader claimed that he had flown 300 m on 14 October 1897, and also that he had made a second test with the *Éole* on an 800-m straight track at Satory in September 1891, with a new boiler fitted, and had become airborne for about 100 m before striking some wagons and being damaged. Unfortunately, from the historical viewpoint, there is no evidence to substantiate either claim.

IN ENGLAND IN 1887, expatriate American Hiram Maxim was asked if he thought it was possible to make a flying machine. He replied, 'Certainly; the domestic goose is able to fly and why should not a man be

right
Sir Hiram Maxim's aeroplane was powered by two 180-hp compound engines, the steam for which came from a single boiler with 7,650 gas burner jets.

Crowds gather to see
Maxim's giant aeroplane
at Baldwyn's Park. Despite
its obvious size, this
photograph was taken
before the upper and lower
wing extensions and fore
and aft elevators were
attached, with which wing
span became 31.7 m and
overall length 28.96 m.

able to do so as well as a goose?' Between 1891 and 1894 Maxim spent some £20,000, much of it his own money, on experimental apparatus, the design and construction of two ingenious 180-hp steam engines producing 2.3 kg per hp, 5.43 m-diameter propellers, and the vast airframe itself which made extensive use of welded steel tubing. At the time of its test on 31 July 1894, the machine weighed a staggering 3,629 kg and, with the outer wing panels attached, spanned no less than 31.7 m. It was run along a track 550 m in length, fitted with restraining rails intended to prevent the machine from lifting freely. Although Maxim provided adequate lateral stability by giving the wings acute dihedral, and excessive pendulum stability by positioning the centre of gravity well below the centre of lift, and had fitted fore and aft elevators, he had little conception of the need for lateral control.

During the 31 July trial, Maxim increased the steam pressure until the propellers were registering a thrust of 908 kg, and then released the machine. It soon reached a speed of 67 km/h, when all of the outrigger

below
Damage to the four-crew
structure of Maxim's
aeroplane, and
restraining rails,
following the 31 July
1894 flight.

wheels were engaged on the upper restraining safety rail, indicating that the machine was completely sustained off the ground to a height of 60 cm by its lifting surfaces. Then, one of its outrigger axles failed, a restraining rail broke and a piece caught one of the propellers, forcing Maxim to cut off the steam and let the machine settle. It was severely damaged, but it had covered some 183 m without touching the ground, the last part of this uncontrolled flight being free from restraint. However, Maxim lost the support of his backers.

In 1899 Maxim said that, although his experiments proved that propulsion and lift could be obtained by mechanical means, he never dared trust himself to his machine 'because I could not manage the balance. That is the crux of the question'.

THE MOST CONTROVERSIAL EARLY CLAIMS TO SUBSTANTIAL FLYING SUCCESS centre around the activities of Gustave Weisskopf (Whitehead), a Bavarian domiciled in the USA. Whitehead is said to have made a

flight of several hundred metres at a height of 15 m at Bridgeport, Connecticut, at 2 a.m. on the night of 14 August 1901, using an acetylene-powered monoplane that had powered wheels as well as powered propellers. Equally controversially, on 17 January 1902 he is said to have made two circular flights over Long Island Sound, one covering 3.2 km and the other 12 km, in a kerosene-powered, twin-engined flying-boat which used components taken from his earlier landplane, and supposedly alighted on the Sound.

A preliminary study of these aircraft shows that they were impractical and almost certainly incapable of making a sustained flight of great duration. Further, their controllability is open to question, there are no reliable eyewitness accounts contemporary with the events and the belated affidavits gathered by proponents are often contradictory.

Recently, tentative hops have been made by 'replicas', but these have little bearing on the claims, since they differ from the originals in essential details, so the fact that they left the ground does not prove in any certain way that their forebears did so. Curiously, Whitehead subsequently regressed to elementary Chanute-type hang-gliders.

PERHAPS THE MOST UNFORTUNATE PRE-WRIGHT PIONEER was the Austrian Wilhelm Kress, a piano maker turned mature engineer who, at 65 years of age, ended his experiments clinging for life in the water at the Tullnerbach reservoir, having been on the very edge of proper flight. Only a stone groyne had stood between success and failure.

Kress had devised a remarkable tandem-wing monoplane with three sets of wings, each set carried above the fuselage at different heights. The airframe was constructed mainly of steel tubes – except for wooden wing ribs – and rested on twin pontoons made from aluminium sheets which suited it to operations from snow or water. Although he had calculated the need for a 40-hp engine weighing 200 kg, the specification proved impossible to meet and the delivered engine offered only 30 hp for a weight of 380 kg. With this fitted, the aircraft had a serious all-up weight problem.

When launched, the seaplane sank further into the water than anticipated, and its stability was also badly affected. Nevertheless, after a number of taxiing trials, Kress prepared for flight. Despite its weight, as the seaplane gathered speed the pontoons began to raise from their depths but, just as flight seemed guaranteed, Kress had to stop the engine and turn sharply to avoid the wall, allowing the wind to flip the machine, which then sank.

Although restoration was put in hand in 1902, it was never completed. Some claims are made that he had actually left the water before capsizing, others said that he did not. It is generally accepted, however, that he probably did rise briefly and as such his remarkable aircraft was the first piloted petrol-driven aeroplane to fly and the first to 'hop' from water.

right
Wilhelm Kress poses beside his partially completed tandem-triplane seaplane *c.* 1899. Trials began in October 1901, on the Tullnerbach reservoir, after a lengthy wait for delivery of the engine. The seaplane was the first petrol engine-driven aeroplane to 'fly' (see the main text).

above

Professor Samuel
Pierpont Langley (right)
and his chief assistant,
Charles Manly who
not only developed
an outstanding 52-hp
aero-engine but piloted
the full-size *Aerodrome*.
The Langely-Manly
team, like Kress, so
nearly beat the Wright
brothers to the accolade
of making the world's
first sustained and
manned aeroplane flight.

RICHARD WILLIAM PEARSE of New Zealand is another serious contender for beating the Wrights into the air, as his bamboo and aluminium monoplane fitted with a two-cylinder, horizontally-opposed engine of his own design definitely flew in front of witnesses on or about 31 March 1903. This took place from level ground and covered a distance of about 50 m, before the machine crashed into a hedge. However, such a flight can hardly be considered 'sustained', the aircraft was not demonstrably controllable, and it landed on ground lower than the point of take-off. Nonetheless, despite these caveats, it was a genuine flight, which makes it important, and the first 'hop' flight in New Zealand. Similarly, the German, Carl Jatho, managed a 'hop' flight in his aeroplane on 18 August 1903, the recorded distance of just 18 m being due in part to the serious lack of power from the 9-hp engine.

IN THE USA, TWO RIVAL PROGRAMMES OF PAINSTAKING EXPERIMENTATION AND RESEARCH WERE CULMINATING IN A PHOTO FINISH IN THE QUEST TO FLY, that of Professor Samuel Pierpont Langley having the added advantage of massive government financial backing. Langley, the accomplished American astronomer, mathematician and physicist, who became third secretary of the Smithsonian Institution in November 1887, first undertook a series of power-to-weight ratio and aerodynamic experiments between 1887 and 1891. He initially used a steam-powered whirling table apparatus which he constructed at Allegheny, and thereafter tested 30 to 40 small flying models of various configurations from monoplanes to biplanes and tandem wing designs, powered by twisted rubber strands. Not until March 1891 was a model produced that was sufficiently light to fly. However, Langley decided that larger models with a better power source were required to further his work. Although he realised that control would also pose major problems, his preoccupation with light structures and efficient engines distracted him from this vital issue.

The first of the large flying models or *Aerodromes* as he called them, the No 0, completed in the spring of 1892, was a steam-powered aircraft using twin pusher propellers. Overweight, underpowered and structurally weak, it was not even tested. Nor were the next two models. The fourth model was still underpowered, but the next, the No 4, seemed more promising. After modification, this machine, and the following, No 5, were catapult-launched from a houseboat on the Potomac River in October 1894, and short-duration flights were achieved.

below
Langley's steam-driven
Aerodrome No 6,
modified from No 4,
which flew for one
minute and 45 seconds
on 28 November 1896.
Such a flight on just one
horsepower seemed to
almost guarantee that a
piloted full-scale version
with a powerful petrol
engine would prove
highly successful.

Langley quickly realised that major changes were needed if improved flights were to be made. Problems to overcome included devising wings that could withstand catapult-launching without distortion and yet be sufficiently light in weight, and stability needed improving. Thus, his last two models reappeared with new tandem wings and complementary cruciform tail surfaces. Indeed, No 4 had changed so much that it was renumbered No 6.

On 6 May 1896 the modified No 5, with a 4-m wing span and a Langley-designed steam engine, made a magnificent flight of 1,006 m at a speed of 32 to 40 km/h, during which it flew large circles and gained altitude before the steam power ran out and the model began a shallow glide downwards, landing without damage on the water. This flight was followed by another of 700 m. This was the first time in history that a large powered model had managed a truly sustained flight. But this was just the start. On 28 November the No 6 model accomplished 1,280 m at a speed of 48 km/h, flying for one minute and forty-five seconds, and all on just one hp from its steam engine.

Entirely satisfied with the results of his experiments, in 1897 Langley asserted that within two or three years, if given the finance, he could build a man-carrying *Aerodrome* capable of a four-hour flight, although it appears he had little ambition to continue towards this end. However, the outbreak of the Spanish–American war in 1899, and President McKinley's interest in the programme following the report of a special commission, ignited official support and duly the US Board of Ordnance and Fortification awarded Langley a grant of $25,000 towards the construction of the full-size machine, with a further $25,000 to follow if the programme was deemed to be on track.

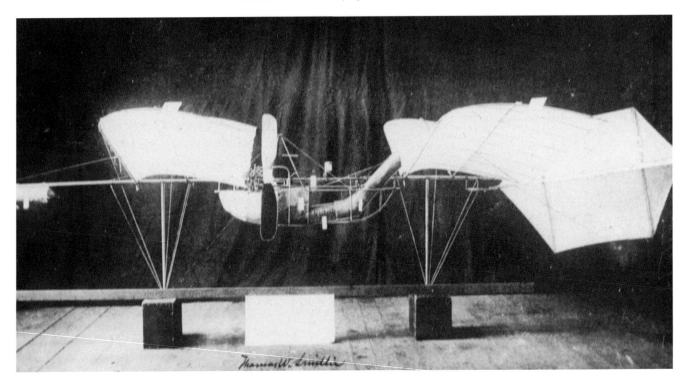

With this backing, progress towards manned experiments was rapid, as Langley already considered he had a good airframe design. It was a suitable engine that now posed the biggest problem, as a steam engine was a non-starter. In 1898 Langley contracted Stephen Balzer to develop a suitable petrol engine; Balzer had already produced a petrol motorcar engine. However, the resulting rotary engine was seriously underpowered for use on the full-size aircraft, and so in August 1900 Charles Manly, Langley's chief assistant, took over engine development and modified the basic Balzer design to become a five-cylinder static radial weighing only 154 kg, taking power output from just 8 hp to an incredible 52 hp. Unfortunately, this wonderful achievement took time and it was not until March 1903 that all was ready, so delaying trials with the full-size *Aerodrome*.

The airframe for this had been completed by early September 1900, awaiting only the engine. Fortunately, the intervening time had not been entirely wasted. A quarter-scale flying model had been built several months earlier than the full-scale airframe, and this was used for flight testing with a 3.2-hp petrol engine. In June 1901 this scale craft made four short and fairly poor flights, but still demonstrated the general stability of the design. Continued work on the scale *Aerodrome* was eventually rewarded, however, with a good flight in 1903. But, by this time, the $50,000 had been spent and a further $23,000, from three different funds, had also been absorbed and the full-size *Aerodrome* had yet to be flown.

On 7 October 1903 the 14.6 m-span full-size *Aerodrome*, with Manly at the controls, at long last accelerated along the 21-m catapult track with a new launching mechanism on top of the houseboat, ready to make the long-anticipated manned flight. However, instead of flying straight and steady as had the models, the machine fouled the launcher and plunged into the water 'like a handful of mortar'. After extensive repairs, a second attempt was made, on 8 December. This time the *Aerodrome* broke up on launch, the rear wings collapsing, causing the *Aerodrome* to nose up vertically before plunging into the Potomac. Manly survived the crash.

In retrospect, it can be argued that Langley's beautifully crafted aeroplane had several inherent shortcomings, including possessing a structure that could not withstand the stress of a catapult launch

above
Orville Wright
photographed at Dayton,
Ohio, in 1909.

and a control system that was completely inadequate and untested, whilst little thought had been given to the problem of effecting a truly safe landing. But, most of all, the launch method had been an unwise choice.

With the funding gone, and seeing the Wright brothers grasp the very prize that had slipped from his fingers, Langley, a discouraged man, died in February 1906. Yet his achievements had been many, including having produced the first-ever unmanned, heavier-than-air aircraft to demonstrate a truly sustained flight (model No 5), and the first aeroplane to make a sustained flight on the power of a petrol engine (the quarter-scale model). It can also be said that he produced the first man-carrying aeroplane to be capable of sustained flight (the full-size *Aerodrome*), although this was not achieved. This final accolade is not without merit, for in 1914 the full-size *Aerodrome* was restored by Glenn Curtiss in order to fight a legal injunction over patents filed against his company by the Wright Aeronautical Company. Although converted into a seaplane for flight testing in 1914, it was otherwise virtually original and it lifted from the water perfectly well on 28 May that year!

above
Wilbur Wright with the
new Model A two-seater
at Auvours in France
where, between
September and
December 1908, he
established a series
of new world distance
records for aeroplanes
by flying 66.6 km,
99.8 km and 124.7 km.

NOW, IT WAS TIME FOR THE WRIGHTS TO TRY THEIR LUCK. Orville and Wilbur Wright might, to some, have seemed unlikely men to make the greatest contribution to aeronautics of their generation, and in doing so kick-start a complete industry. Respected sons of a bishop and running a bicycle firm in Dayton, Ohio, it was Wilbur who sparked their interest in aviation, having read about the achievements of Otto Lilienthal, and wondered whether they could carry on from where Lilienthal's untimely death had left exploitation of the air.

The brothers began their researches as a pastime, but their keen eye for detail and methodology soon brought purpose to the project. Like most great men before them, including da Vinci, they were willing to learn from others and build upon established knowledge. Thus, they struck up a friendship with Octave Chanute, a man willing to encourage all comers and share his findings, which resulted in the Wrights' bias towards biplanes with superimposed wings and crossed wire bracing. But, for flight control, Wilbur conceived, as a separate issue, the idea of wing warping from watching buzzards correct lateral balance by torsion of their wingtips. This was an important observation, although it should be noted that Lilienthal

right
The Wright brothers
flying their No 1 glider
as a tethered kite
at Kitty Hawk, in
September 1900. No 1
could also be flown as
a manned kite and in
manned free glides.

had previously come to a similar conclusion after years of using the more basic 'pilot weight-shift' form of control on his gliders. Moreover, as any future powered aircraft would become larger and heavier than existing gliders, weight shift control was clearly not a consideration.

Virtually from the outset the Wrights had powered flying as their ultimate goal, but to achieve this they had to go through the same stages of airframe development as had earlier pioneers. However, unlike so many of the forerunners, they recognised the need to tackle the tricky problem of flight control as an immediate issue, not as an afterthought, as only by surviving their flying experiments would they achieve their ambitions! Safe flying in a safe craft, with flying skills learned slowly and progressively, was clearly the way forward. Only then, after airframe and control had been mastered, would they concern themselves about suitable engine power.

The obvious first stage was to construct a glider, initially a small unmanned test vehicle, merely for their experiments with wing warping. The resulting 1.52-m biplane of August 1899 was an adaptable vehicle to be flown as a kite, on which wing stagger could be altered and the horizontal stabiliser could be mounted at the front or rear.

Once satisfied with their lateral and longitudinal control experiments, they built at very little cost a new full-size biplane with a 5.2-m span and large front elevator, having an all-up weight of just 23.5 kg. Having rejected weight-shift control, the pilot on this craft was able to adopt a drag-reducing prone position on the lower wing, controlling wing warping by tightening wires to twist the wingtips, thereby producing similar aerodynamic effects to modern ailerons. And, just as Lilienthal had protected himself by fitting his gliders with a willow hoop to absorb the impact from a nose-first accident, so the Wrights considered the forward elevator had the secondary task of pilot protection.

Ready in 1900 as glider No 1, the brothers sought advice as to where best to fly, the Weather Bureau recommending a place called Kitty Hawk for its constant winds and soft sands. There, No 1 was flown principally as an unpiloted tethered kite, although it was also used as a manned kite and in free glides. For some of the tests No 1 was rigged with wing dihedral to give inherent stability, but in this form it flew poorly in gusty conditions.

Happy with the results, the brothers set about building glider No 2 with wings of 6.7-m span, almost double the surface area of No 1, camber and anhedral droop. A foot-operated bar engaged warp. This was taken to Kill Devil Hills, south of Kitty Hawk, for trials in 1901, where initially it proved a disappointment. But, after reducing wing camber, flights of up to 119 m were demonstrated, while control was possible in 26-knot winds. However, the glider had a tendency to pitch up and stall, while the lift generated by the wings was far less than had been calculated.

This was a defining moment for the brothers, as it dawned on them that the tables they had used to calculate lift, produced by Lilienthal, were not entirely accurate. So Wilbur and Orville set about an intensive ten-month programme of original research which was to give them an unassailable lead in aeronautics for years to come. Initial use of a bicycle rig to compare the drag of a flat plate with that of various aerofoils was not particularly successful, and so they constructed a basic wind tunnel from a box and fan. This proved excellent and provided accurate data on air pressures, and the aerodynamic properties of aerofoils and control surfaces. More than 200 wing sections were tested in two months in

below
Wright No 3 glider after
having the twin rear fins
replaced by a single
rudder that was
activated by the wing
warping mechanism.
Thereby, the warp drag
was countered by the
movement of the rudder,
allowing smooth banking
and levelling. It was
highly successful.

various monoplane, biplane and triplane configurations.

Using this data, glider No 3 was constructed in the summer of 1902, featuring slender varying camber wings and a new hip-effected method of wing warping. Their largest aircraft to date, with a span of 9.75 m and area of 28.34 sq m, it also featured twin rear fins.

Trials with No 3 began in September. However, although flying well, when the wings were warped it demonstrated a tendency to enter a spin. Furthermore, during side slips the twin fins encouraged the wings to rotate about their vertical axis. The answer came in replacing the twin fins with a single movable rudder that was activated by the warping mechanism. This solution was perfect, with the warp drag cancelled out by the movement of the rudder. Smooth banking and levelling became possible. Hundreds of controlled flights followed, one lasting 26 seconds and covering 190 m. They returned home, leaving No 3 at the base.

below
Probably the most famous photograph in the history of aviation, showing Orville Wright leaving the launch track at the start of the *Flyer*'s 12 second undulating flight on 17 December 1903, with Wilbur looking on. Three more flights took place that day, the last by Wilbur covering 260 m.

With airframe configuration and control method under their belts, their attention turned to the tricky problem of power. The answer, as before, lay in their own hands, and over a six-week period they designed and constructed a 12-hp internal combustion engine weighing 77 kg, and twin geared-down propellers to go with it, the latter to be driven by bicycle chains. Now the countdown to a manned and powered flight began, but with Langley seeming just as likely to get there first.

The first Wright powered aeroplane was aptly named *Flyer*, its 12.2-m wing span giving it an area of 47.38 sq m. The machine, without pilot, weighed 274 kg. The engine was mounted offset of centre on the lower wing and, to compensate, the starboard wings were slightly longer to generate extra lift.

In September 1903, the Wrights returned to Kill Devil Hills with *Flyer*, only to find the base in chaos and No 3 damaged. This was a body-blow, as they wanted to renew their flying skills on the glider before attempting a powered flight. Although time was of the essence, No 3 was repaired and flown that

below
This photograph of a Wright two-seater in July 1908 shows how the driving chain crossed on this side of the aircraft to reverse the direction of the propeller spin, while the propeller itself and its shaft had still to be attached.

October. But more problems lay in store. When *Flyer*'s engine was started for the first time, it backfired and a propeller shaft was bent. Hurriedly, new shafts were sent for, arriving on 20 November, but these proved to be structurally weak. In exasperation, Orville went home to make new shafts for himself. While away, Langley tried and failed for the second time to launch his full-size *Aerodrome*, which Orville heard about only as he returned to Kitty Hawk.

By 14 December *Flyer* had been repaired and made ready for testing. A flick of a coin put Wilbur at the controls of the aeroplane, which rested on a bicycle hub trolley on the launching track. The wind being light, *Flyer* moved ahead quickly and lifted, but Wilbur pulled up too sharply and stalled the aircraft, which descended to the sand after three and a half seconds in the air, catching a wing and slewing around. The elevator and a skid were damaged and required repair.

This attempt had used a sloping launch track because the wind had been light. Two days later, similar light winds dashed hopes to fly again, but on 17 December Orville mounted the *Flyer* as it rested on the track that had been repositioned to level ground, the wind being strong on this bitterly cold winter's morning. As personnel from the Kill Devil Life Saving Station and others stood by, the engine pre-warmed, at 10.35 a.m. the restraining wire was released. This time *Flyer* made slow progress into the strong wind, with Wilbur running alongside to help steady the machine as it gathered speed along the track. After a distance of about 12 m the *Flyer* lifted and flew for 12 historic seconds, its slow undulating progress to a height of about 3 m and then dive for the ground continuing over a distance of 37 m from take-off point, ending with another sudden dive. Orville had fought with the over-sensitive elevator to keep the machine in level flight under windy conditions, but had over-compensated.

If the day's flying had ended then, it is unlikely that 17 December 1903 would be recorded in history as marking the first-ever flight by a manned, powered and controllable aeroplane. Twelve seconds was hardly a flight at all and, as for control, well!

Fortunately, after minor repairs, the *Flyer* made three more flights that day, the next by Wilbur being almost an exact repeat of the first in terms of undulation and time in the air (about one second longer), although an additional 23 m was covered due to the lighter wind. The third flight, by Orville, was dramatic, as a gust of wind from the starboard side raised the *Flyer* and pitched it to port, requiring Orville to use warping to regain lateral stability. The wing warping proved very effective, and as Orville tried to land the starboard wing touched the ground first due to his over-compensation, ending a terrifying flight of 15 seconds and some 61 m distance.

Wilbur took the controls for the fourth flight at 12 a.m. Once in the air, the aircraft again pitched up and down before coming under control for at least half the distance flown, although ending in a now-characteristic groundward dive. The distance covered had been a wonderful 260 m, during 59 seconds in the air. It was a triumph. Unfortunately, it was also to be the *Flyer*'s last-ever flight. Having been taken back to base, it was overturned by strong winds and damaged beyond repair.

Ironically, a few days later the Wrights received a letter from industrialist Godfrey Cabot, asking whether their aircraft could be used to fly huge quantities of freight over a 16-mile route in West Virginia. Cabot was seven years too early in his plans, as it was not until 7 November 1910 that the first-ever freight was carried by aeroplane, but on that historic occasion it was again a Wright machine that proved capable of the task in hand, a much- improved Model B that transported 488 m of silk in two packages for the Morehouse-Martins Company, flying between Dayton and Columbus. Although a publicity stunt costing Morehouse-Martins an incredible $5,000, the company still made more than a $1,000 profit, having sold some of the silk as tiny pieces mounted on postcards to mark the event.

Orville Wright judged the *Flyer* as a success because it had taken off under its own power, flown forwards without loss of speed and landed safely at a point that was as high as the starting position, reasonable definitions that clearly defined the differences between successful gliding and powered flights. But, as already noted, some earlier aircraft had, indeed, already met these criteria. So why does history still reward the Wrights? The reality is that the *Flyer* was the first-ever manned and powered aeroplane to make a flight of any genuine significance and duration, and that in its design and development potential it far surpassed anything that had gone before. Therefore, if it requires the additional conditions of *controlled* and *sustained* to keep it as the historical 'first', so be it, for no other aeroplane deserves the accolade more.

IN SEPTEMBER 1903, BEFORE *FLYER* HAD TAKEN TO THE AIR, WILBUR HAD SENT A LETTER TO HIS FATHER STATING THAT 'I THINK THERE IS A SLIGHT POSSIBILITY OF ACHIEVING FAME AND FORTUNE FROM IT'. Back at home in December 1903 for family celebrations, it was time to reflect and plan new exploits. After all, this was only to be the beginning!

Flyer II was the 1904 model for trials from Simms Station, making 105 flights from 26 May. On 15 September it demonstrated its controllability by performing the first turn, followed five days later by the first one-kilometre flight during which it flew the first closed circuit, on each occasion with Wilbur at the controls. Then, on 9 November, it flew for a remarkable 4.43 km, staying up for just over five minutes.

Flyer III for 1905 was given a 25-hp engine and first flew on 23 June. This is recognised as having been the first entirely practical model. Fully controllable, it flew an amazing 39 km around a circuit in 38 minutes on 5 October; nobody else was yet ready to fly for more than a few seconds. But, just 11 days later, at the very pinnacle of their success, they stopped flying altogether in order to protect the confidentiality of their invention and exploit the business side. The French government, still extolling Ader as the first to fly, was vigorous in its attempts to purchase the rights to the Wright aircraft, as were others.

It was not until 1907 that the Wrights began new experiments, and not until May 1908 that they resumed flying, by which time they had squandered their staggering technological lead. By August 1908 Wilbur was flying the new Model A two-seater at Le Mans, France, while Orville concentrated on the

above

Discussions between the Wright brothers and the US Army over a military aeroplane first took place in early 1905, but were not fruitful. However, on 23 December 1907 the US Army issued the first-ever specification for a military aeroplane for commercial tender. On 10 February 1908 the Army signed contracts with the Wright brothers, Augustas Herring and J. Scott, but only the Wright Model A was delivered. Trials began at Fort Myer, Virginia, on 3 September that year. The accident on 17 September that injured Orville and killed Lt Selfridge, meant that it took until 27 July 1909 for a Model A to pass the first official test – an endurance of over one hour – when Orville and Lt Frank Lahm flew for one hour 12 minutes and 20 seconds.

forthcoming US military trials at Fort Myer, Virginia. Individual Wright aircraft were built at Dayton, with those subsequently destined for European purchasers being sent in 'knock-down' form and reassembled at Pau in France, where Wilbur went to take advantage of improved weather conditions.

Meanwhile, in Britain in late 1908, members of the Aero Club had formed a syndicate in the hope of purchasing UK patent rights to the Wright Model A, but the UK market was seen as too small by the Americans, who refused. However, in February 1909 the rights to construct six machines was finally granted. Short Brothers became the chosen manufacturer in England and a contract was signed that March; these became the very first aeroplanes to be built on a production line anywhere in the world. A new industry had been inaugurated. Selling rights and licences became the Wright brothers' chosen main commercial route, and even in their home country a group of investors founded Wright & Company in November 1909, with the brothers selling patent rights and undertaking a major technical role within the company.

The Wright brothers themselves recorded other historical 'firsts' during 1908–09 – including carrying the first aeroplane passenger (Charles Furnas on 14 May 1908; see also the next chapter for the first-ever passenger of a powered aircraft), shooting the first aerial cinematography film from the air (in Italy, on 24 April 1909), and selling the US government its very first military aeroplane (Wright Model A, named *Miss Columbia*, on 2 August 1909) – but their best days had passed.

As with the Montgolfier brothers, the Wrights' legacy to aeronautics was astonishing and their fame assured, but their time of unrivalled aerial mastery had been unnecessarily curtailed by the decision to exploit commercial aspects rather than stay at the very forefront of technology by continued research, development and adaptation. Wilbur died in 1912 of typhoid fever, whilst Orville saw one of the last Wright aeroplanes going to the US Navy in 1914, still using wing-warping and chain drive. In the following year Wright & Company was sold. Orville lived long enough to see the world through two World Wars that used aeroplanes in vast numbers.

Aviation at Full Power

below

A depiction of Blanchard and Jeffries' flight across the English Channel in 1785. Jeffries, having heard of Blanchard's intended journey, offered to pay for the ascent in return for accompanying the Frenchman. With little forethought as to the suitability of the balloon and equipment for such a two-man flight, they were forced to throw overboard the bags of ballast, the two anchors, the steering oars, rudder and windlass, leaflets and mail, basket ornaments, the cork life jackets, bags containing their urine, and even most of their clothes to prevent an early descent into the water.

WHILST MEANINGFUL POWERED AEROPLANE FLIGHT HAD ELUDED THE NINETEENTH-CENTURY PIONEERS, lighter-than-air flying had progressed apace. Balloons had got man airborne in ascending flight at the end of the eighteenth century, but the vagaries of the wind meant that their uses were severely limited to pleasure and tethered observation. Attempts to rectify this had been swift, indeed as early as October 1784,

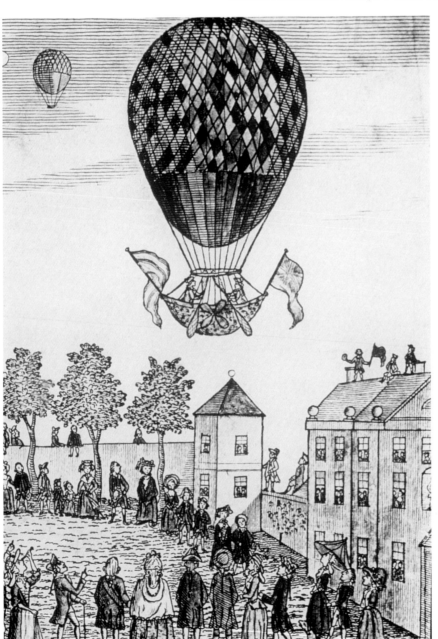

Frenchman Jean-Pierre Blanchard had tried to control the flight of a balloon by mounting a hand-operated six-blade propeller to the basket. It was totally ineffectual. Nevertheless, Blanchard himself became one of the great names in ballooning, remembered for making the first flight across the English Channel, on 7 January 1785, in a hydrogen balloon (with American, Dr John Jeffries), and being responsible for making the first balloon flights in the Netherlands, Germany and Belgium, plus the first free-flight in the USA.

In the same year that Blanchard tried to add 'power' to a balloon, Lt Jean-Baptiste Marie Meusnier of the French Corps of Engineers published a design for a dirigible, or steerable airship. This was never constructed, but the design had, for the first time, the cigar shape that was to become standard for most later airships. It also featured inner and outer envelopes to maintain the overall shape even after gas was released. Its Achilles' heel would have been its power source, intended initially to be 80 crew turning three very large propellers.

Similar thinking drove the Robert brothers who, on 15 July 1784, flew an airship (cylindrical, this time) fitted with a ballonet, an important milestone. The ballonet was basically a gastight compartment within the main envelope that could be inflated with air, or deflated, to vary altitude. Ballonets subsequently came into common use to maintain envelope shape during changes in lifting gas volume, and to adjust trim, and they are still present today in airships.

The lack of a suitable engine now held up

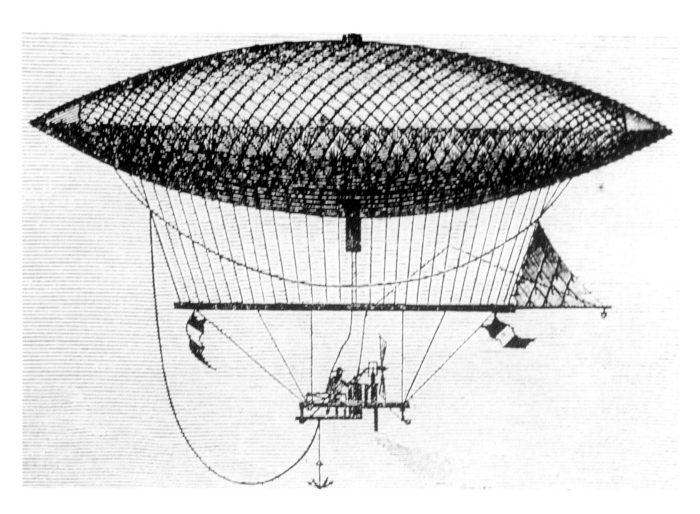

above

Henry Giffard's
remarkable dirigible of
1852, the first in history
to make a manned and
powered flight.
Constructed with the
help of Sciama and
David, it was driven at
slow speed by a 3-hp
steam engine weighing
150 kg empty, turning a
3.3 m diameter three-
blade propeller at 110
revolutions a minute.

airship development in general, for, without such a power source, an airship was merely a cumbersome and over-sized balloon. Indeed, it would be nearly 60 years before the very first manned and powered airship flight in history could take place, but when it did it was certainly worth the wait. On 24 September 1852 Frenchman Henry Giffard flew between the Paris Hippodrome and Trappes. Incredibly, this was not only an historic event for airships, it also marked the first powered and sustained flight by any type of manned aircraft. At just 8 km/h, Giffard's 27-km journey was hardly speedy, as the 44-m craft relied on only 3 hp from its steam engine. Twenty years later, Austrian Paul Hänlein became the first person to install an internal combustion engine on an airship, the 5-hp, four-cylinder engine being fuelled by gas taken from the envelope. Unfortunately, lack of funds meant that development of this airship stopped after tethered flights.

It was again in France that the very first fully controllable, powered airship appeared, appropriately named *La France*, which made an 8-km circular flight from and to Chalais-Meudon on 9 August 1884. Flown by Capt Charles Renard and Lt Arthur Krebs, it managed a respectable 23 km/h during the 23-minute

below
Santos-Dumont's airship
No 6 rounds the Eiffel
Tower.

journey, powered by a 9-hp Gramme electric motor. Then, Dr Karl Wölfert, the great German pioneer, devised the first dirigible to mount a petrol engine (a 2-hp Daimler), which flew on 12 August 1888. Tragically, in 1897 Dr Wölfert and his mechanic lost their lives, the first to an accident involving an airship. Wölfert had, though, established a German interest that was to have grave repercussions early in the next century.

A RATHER UNIQUE DEMONSTRATION OF CONTROLLED AIRSHIP FLYING took place on 19 October 1901, when Brazilian-born Alberto Santos-Dumont piloted his 20-hp petrol-engined No 6 airship around the Eiffel Tower in Paris. This grand journey won the Deutsch prize of 100,000 francs for the first flight from the Aéro-Club de France's park at Saint-Cloud, around the Tower and return in under 30 minutes; he had taken 29 minutes and 30 seconds.

Written histories on aviation often claim this to be the first flight around the Eiffel Tower. Not so. Santos-Dumont had earlier constructed his No 5 airship for the task, and on 12 July 1901 had made three flights from Longchamp Hippodrome, the first reaching the district of Puteaux and back, the second was an actual attempt to circumnavigate the Tower but Santos-Dumont alighted at the Trocadero Gardens due to a broken steering rudder cable, and the third from the Gardens, around the Tower and back to Longchamp. After this flight Santos-Dumont declared that the problems of the dirigible had been resolved.

The following day, Santos-Dumont made another attempt to comply with the rules of the Deutsch prize. He completed the journey in 40 minutes, but came down in trees at Baron de Rothschild's park. After repair and testing, on 8 August he again rounded the Tower, but a gas leak and engine problem brought him down violently on a house at the Trocadero, leaving the airship hanging in shreds. Santos-Dumont survived by hanging from the airship's ropes until rescued by firemen.

SANTOS-DUMONT, AN AVID AVIATOR AND EXPERIMENTER, CONTINUED TO DEVELOP AIRSHIPS alongside a new passion for heavier-than-air craft, including (initially) the helicopter which he soon abandoned. His powered aeroplane was completed in 1906 as a tail-first cellular box-kite with substantial wing dihedral, with a cellular canard structure mounted in front to combine the functions of rudder and elevator, thereby seemingly to fly backwards! To get some understanding of control, he first attached the aeroplane to the underside of his new No 14 airship, which lifted machine and pilot into the air for tethered checks. Thus, the aeroplane became the 14-bis. The original 24-hp Antoinette engine was later replaced by a 50-hp version, with metal pusher propeller. The entire aeroplane weighed 300 kg.

On 14 October 1906 the Fédération Aéronautique Internationale was founded in France, becoming the international regulatory body for aeronautical achievements. Only nine days earlier Wilbur Wright had flown 39 km in *Flyer III*, but this had preceded establishment of the FAI and so could not have been officially witnessed by the organisation. And so, one of the strangest quirks in aviation history was about to take place.

Santos-Dumont put 14-bis forward to take part in two major competitions, both aimed at progressing the art of heavier-than-air flying in Europe. The first, with a prize of 1,500 francs and organised by the Aéro-Club, was for the first aeroplane to fly 100 m, with a maximum descent rate of 10 per cent, while the Archdeacon Cup was less ambitious and offered 3,000 francs to a machine capable of only 25 m and with a maximum descent rate of 25 per cent.

Mounting his 14-bis on 13 September 1906, at Bagatelle meadows near Paris, Santos-Dumont made a tiny 'hop' flight of some 7 m, breaking struts and the propeller on landing. It was repaired and then, on 23 October, 14-bis covered a distance of 65 m, rising to a height of 3 m, this time damaging the undercarriage. But, at least, 14-bis had flown comfortably and won the Archdeacon Cup. After adding hexagonal ailerons within the outer cells of the wings, on 12 November Santos-Dumont managed six flights, the last covering 220 m during just over 21 seconds in the air, winning the Aéro-Club prize and in doing so also recording the first sustained flight in Europe by a powered and manned aeroplane.

Witnessed by the FAI, Santos-Dumont's flight of 220 m thereby became the very first world absolute distance record achieved by a manned and powered aeroplane, standing until Frenchman Henry Farman flew his Voisin over 771 m in October 1907. This complete nonsense of aviation meant that Wilbur Wright's 38 minutes in the air in 1905 and the 1906 flight had been ignored as a world record in favour of Santos-Dumont's witnessed 21 seconds of 1906. To complicate history further, it should be realised that on 12 September 1906, Danish engineer Jacob Ellehammer had flown his biplane over a distance of 43 m at Lindholm, so pre-dating Santos-Dumont's achievement. However, on this occasion Ellehammer's biplane had been tethered to a post to permit a circular flight around a 300-m track and, as such, was 'uncontrollable' by the pilot and therefore is discounted as the first sustained flight in Europe. Interestingly, on 13 January 1908 Farman flew his Voisin biplane on the first free-flying circuit flight in Europe, winning the 50,000-franc prize offered by Henry

Deutsch de la Meurthe and Ernest Archdeacon for the first witnessed one-kilometre flight in Europe, which took Farman one minute and 28 seconds to complete. Then, on 29 May, Archdeacon flew with Farman, becoming the first European passenger.

Although originally marginalised by the FAI, it took Wilbur Wright only until 21 September 1908 to break the FAI's then-standing official world distance record for a powered aeroplane, covering 66.6 km at Camp d'Auvours; previously, on 20 May, Frenchman Paul Tissandier had established the first FAI absolute speed record at Pau, flying a Wright biplane at 54.77 km/h. The 21 September flight is viewed as important for several reasons, not least as it is said to have been the first-ever fully significant endurance flight by an aeroplane. However, the prior FAI record, set by Léon Delagrange in a Voisin biplane four days earlier, had covered a very respectable 24.1 km and this demonstrated in a real way that European aeroplanes had closed the technology gap with the Wright biplanes. After Wilbur flew nearly 125 km on 31 December, Wright biplanes faded from the FAI distance and speed records for good, only reappearing occasionally for altitude records.

RETURNING TO OCTOBER 1907, THE FAMED INVENTOR DR ALEXANDER GRAHAM BELL then co-founded the Aerial Experiment Association in the USA, his fellow members including Glenn Hammond Curtiss and Lt Thomas Etholen Selfridge of the US Army Signal Corps. Selfridge became the pilot on Bell's extraordinary and huge *Cygnet I* tetrahedral-cell 'aerodrome' kite, which was first towed into the air by motorboat on 3 December 1907; it was wrecked three days later, with Selfridge walking away unhurt. More importantly,

Selfridge was responsible for designing the Aerial Experiment Association's first powered aeroplane to fly successfully, the *Red Wing*, which flew on 12 March 1908 with Canadian 'Casey' Baldwin at the controls, covering a distance of about 90 m. Tragically, however, Selfridge later became the first-ever fatality of a powered aeroplane accident when, on 17 September 1908, the Wright biplane being flown by Orville Wright at Fort Myer, in which Selfridge was passenger, crashed during US Army military acceptance trials.

Meantime, Glenn Curtiss had founded his original Curtiss Aeroplane Co. on 30 November 1907, the first such company in the USA, having already supplied engines to other pioneers for both lighter-than-air and heavier-than-air purposes. CAC continued as an engine supplier to AEA members, and also provided airframes, while Curtiss's own *June Bug* biplane flew 386 m on 20 June 1908, making him the first American to fly a powered aeroplane after the Wright brothers. Fourteen days later Curtiss managed 1,550 m in *June Bug* during one minute and 42 seconds in the air, winning the *Scientific American* trophy for the first official public flight in the USA of more than one kilometre.

In March 1909 Curtiss and Augustus Herring formed the Herring-Curtiss Company, and then the new Curtiss Aeroplane Company was founded in December 1910, followed by the separate Curtiss Motor Company in December 1911, these merging into the Curtiss Aeroplane & Motor Corporation in 1916. With various subsidiaries and name changes, this company subsequently became the world's largest aircraft company, turning out military and civil aircraft until its heyday ended after World War II.

WITH FRANCE HAVING BECOME THE MOST AERONAUTICALLY-MINDED COUNTRY IN THE WORLD by late 1908, it was perhaps fitting that a Frenchman would make the most revered aeroplane flight since the Wright *Flyer* took to the air in 1903 – the conquest of the English Channel. Louis Blériot, well known for his crashes, had begun his aeronautical career by constructing an ornithopter in 1901, which failed to fly. Having joined forces with Gabriel and Charles Voisin, he built a seaplane glider in 1905 as the Blériot Type II. His Type III powered seaplane of 1906 and Type IV were actually constructed by the Voisin brothers who, with Blériot and Ernest Archdeacon, had founded the world's first aeroplane manufacturing company in July 1905, as Ateliers d'Aviation Edouard Surcouf, Blériot et Voisin.

above
Glenn Curtiss piloting
the *June Bug* biplane on
4 July 1908 to win the
Scientific American
trophy.

right
Frenchman Louis Blériot
relaxes with his wife
before attempting to fly
the English Channel.

The Type V of 1907 was Blériot's first success, while his Type VI *Libellule*
was the first aeroplane to have cantilever wings, flying initially on 11 July 1907.
This was followed by the Type VII, Blériot's third full-size monoplane. The Type
VII was important for introducing what later became regarded as the
conventional layout for aeroplanes, comprising a tractor-mounted engine (50-hp
Antoinette in this case), fully covered fuselage with a forward pilot's cockpit,
rear-mounted tail unit, and an undercarriage comprising twin mainwheels plus
a tailwheel. The Type VII managed just six flights from 10 November 1907,
before ending in one of Blériot's famous crashes on 18 December.

On 23 January 1909 the Type XI flew for the first time, destined to become
the most successful monoplane to appear before World War I. It was Blériot's
chosen vehicle to attempt the first-ever long-distance flight over water.

CONQUEST OF THE ENGLISH CHANNEL had been encouraged by the British *Daily
Mail* newspaper, which had offered a £1,000 prize for the first pilot of any
nationality to fly that stretch of water. The *Daily Mail* had previously offered
other financial incentives to encourage aviation, and continued to do so for
a very long time to come.

In the summer of 1909 there were three contenders, all anticipating flights
in the direction of the French Pas-de-Calais to England. Blériot based himself

left
The Blériot-Voisin
partnership brought
about several
aeroplanes, including
glider and powered
seaplanes during
1905–6. The elliptical
wing featured in two
such powered seaplanes
in 1906, the tandem
elliptical version (as
illustrated), which failed
to fly, and a version with
a rear elliptical wing and
conventional biplane
forward wings plus front
elevators, which was
tested on Lake Enghien.

at Les Baraques, while the Comte de Lambert chose Wissant and Hubert Latham settled on Sangatte. In the event, the competition boiled down to two, Latham and Blériot, both with machines of proven ability, both survivors of air crashes, and both ready and willing at similar times.

English-born Latham had very limited flying experience, having taken up the sport in 1908. His greatest strengths were his boldness and his chosen machine, the beautiful Antoinette IV. The Antoinette monoplane was the brainchild of Léon Levavasseur, who had only begun constructing aeroplanes again in 1908, following the failure of his 1903 machine. It had many excellent features, including large wings of reducing thickness and chord towards the tips, a triangular-section fuselage of lattice girder type to provide great strength and was powered by Levavasseur's own Antoinette engine. Indeed, the Antoinette engine in general had been the driving force behind a great many of the exceptional flights made by European aeroplanes, and was the world's first engine to be produced commercially for aeronautics.

In the very early morning of 19 July 1909, Latham took off from Cap Blanc Nez in fine weather conditions – wireless telegraphy had been used for the first time to obtain weather reports. He soon ascended to the magnificent altitude of 300 m. Unfortunately, after some 13 km the engine stopped and he descended safely into the Channel, where he smoked a cigarette on the floating machine while awaiting rescue by the escorting torpedo boat *Harpon*.

While Latham attempted to get his hands on a replacement Antoinette, at 4.41 a.m. on 25 July Louis Blériot took off from Les Baraques in his Type XI to make his bid. After an eventful flight at between 76 and 150 m altitude, at 5.17 a.m. he landed on the Northfall Meadow by Dover Castle, England, so becoming the first man to cross the English Channel by aeroplane. (The very first crossing by air had previously been made on 7 January 1785, by Blanchard and Jeffries, between Dover and Forêt de Felmores, the occupants having had to discard most of their clothes to lighten the balloon during the flight – see illustration, page 68).

Disappointed at being beaten, just a few days later Latham tried again, only to ditch 1.6 km from the English coast, and was rescued unhurt.

below
Crowds were enthralled
by the air racing at the
22–29 August 1909
Reims International
Aviation Meeting, where
23 aeroplanes competed
for cash prizes. Most of
the world's greatest
names took part,
watched by half a
million spectators.

BLÉRIOT'S TRIUMPH BECAME the catalyst for a huge surge in public and official interest in aviation, both civil and military. The world's first international aviation meeting was held at Reims in France on 22–29 August 1909, during which 23 of the 38 aeroplanes entered for cash-prize events managed to fly. Here, Glenn Curtiss flying a Herring-Curtiss biplane and Louis Blériot in one of his monoplanes raised the FAI world speed record progressively to 77 km/h, and Latham established an FAI altitude record of 155 m flying an Antoinette, while from Betheny (the starting point) Frenchman Louis Paulhan, Latham and Henry Farman progressively raised the world distance record to 180 km. Although Great Britain held its first aviation meeting at Doncaster during 15–23 October 1909 – beating the first officially recognised meeting at Blackpool that October – it was not until J. T. C. Moore-Brabazon flew the Short Biplane No 2 on 30 October 1909 that a *Daily Mail* £1,000 prize was won for the first British pilot to complete a one-mile (1.6 km) circuit flight in an all-British aeroplane. The first aeroplane meeting in the USA took place at the Dominguez Field, Los Angeles, on 10 January 1910.

Now, other aviation 'firsts' started to come thick and fast, including Mme la Baronne de Laroche becoming the world's first certificated woman pilot on 8 March 1910, then only the thirty-sixth certificated French pilot. Frenchman Emil Aubrun, flying a Blériot in Argentina, made the first-ever night flights on 10 March 1910, and Frenchman Henri Fabre flew his *Hydravion* at Martigues on 28 March 1910 to record the first proper aeroplane take-off from water. More impressively, on 23 September 1910 Peruvian Georges Chavez flew a Blériot over the Alps between Switzerland and Italy, but was killed on landing.

Commercially, on 18 February 1911 the world's first official government air-mail flight took place, when Frenchman Henri Pequet flew a Humber biplane between Allahabad and Naini Junction in India, carrying some 6,500 letters. A regular air-mail service started four days later in accordance with the Universal Postal Exhibition in Allahabad, with Pequet joined by fellow pilot British Captain W. Windham. US air-mail flights began on 23 October 1911, when Earl Ovington flew a Queen monoplane over a 10-km route from Nassau Boulevard, New York.

above

The somewhat bizarre-looking *Hydravion* at La Mède harbour at Martigues, in which Frenchman Henri Fabre recorded the first-ever proper flight from water on 28 March 1910. Having a wing span of 14 m and overall weight of 475 kg, the floatplane was adequately provided with power by a 50-hp Gnome rotary engine driving a 2.5 m pusher propeller. Fabre's success on the 28th was doubly remarkable as it also marked his first-ever flight as a pilot or passenger. Incredibly, the 500 m managed that day was turned into 6 km the next!

On 1 January 1914 the St Petersburg-Tampa Airboat Line inaugurated the world's first scheduled airline operations by aeroplane, in Florida, USA. Although historically interesting, it had not been the very first air service by a commercial airline. This honour had already gone to Germany's Delag – Die Deutsche Luftschiffahrt Aktiengesellschaft – which had been formed by Count Ferdinand von Zeppelin on 16 November 1909. Between 1910 and November 1913 Delag carried more than 34,000 passengers between German cities using six rigid airships, plus international services from 1912 to Denmark and Sweden.

BY 1912, THE NUMBER OF CERTIFICATED PILOTS WORLD-WIDE had risen to a staggering 2,490. France, not unexpectedly, had the greatest number by far, at 966, while Great Britain had 382, Germany 345, the USA 193, Italy 186 and Russia 162, and with 11 other countries making up the remainder. Russian pilots included Igor Sikorsky, who had begun his powered aircraft experiments with helicopters in 1909, having first constructed a tiny rubber-powered model helicopter at the age of 12. His 1909 twin contra-rotating rotor helicopter failed to fly, and his similar 1910 helicopter only just managed to lift off the ground as an unmanned vehicle. Turning instead to fixed-wing aeroplanes, his first machine also failed but his second of 1910 made a 12-second flight.

From this modest beginning, by 1913 Sikorsky had managed to design and fly the world's first four-engined aeroplane, the *Russky Vityaz* (Russian Knight), better remembered as *Le Grand*. This was an

above

From the huge *Russky Vityaz*, Igor Sikorsky developed the amazingly successful *Ilya Mourometz*, which first flew as a prototype in January 1914. In February 1914 (when this photograph was taken) this four-engined biplane demonstrated that it could carry 16 people in such smooth flight that it was possible to walk safely on top of the enclosed fuselage.

absolute monster by any measure at the time, having a wing span of 28 m and using four 100-hp engines. First airborne for just a few minutes on 13 May 1913, on 2 August that year it demonstrated a one hour and 54 minute flight with no fewer than nine persons on board, all in enclosed accommodation.

From the *Russky Vityaz* Sikorsky evolved the *Ilya Mourometz* four-engined bomber of World War I, which first flew in prototype form in January 1914 and carried 16 people the following month. Although he continued to design both large and small aeroplanes, including remarkable amphibians in the 1920s and 30s, Sikorsky would eventually return to helicopters while living in the USA, starting a helicopter dynasty in the 1940s that was born out of a pre-World War II test vehicle.

THE HELICOPTER, WHICH HAD FASCINATED — AT ONE TIME OR ANOTHER — DA VINCI, CAYLEY, THE WRIGHTS AND SANTOS-DUMONT, among others, is generally thought to be a post-World War II invention, gaining its first real baptism during the Korean War of the early 1950s. The truth is somewhat different. String-pull toys and other models have already been touched upon in earlier chapters, and now the story jumps to man-carrying machines.

In 1906 Wilbur Wright wrote 'Like all novices we began with the helicopter (in childhood), but soon

Carl Zenker's *Bremen I* helicopter which, although unable to fly, had taken a long time to construct and was a somewhat more considered attempt to produce a successful vertical flying machine than many others of the period.

saw that it had no future and dropped it. The helicopter does with great labor only what the balloon does without labor.' He continued: 'The helicopter is much easier to design than the aeroplane but it is worthless when done.' Perhaps Wilbur should have asked the opinion of those who continued to experiment along the path of vertical heavier-than-air flight.

With our modern knowledge of helicopters, and their great value and versatility, it is all too easy to mock Wilbur's words. But, given the lack of progress with helicopters by 1906, compared to aeroplanes, the future must have appeared bleak. Yet, there had been the odd beacon of inspiration among the many   ill-conceived and aerodynamically flawed projects. One was the *Bremen 1*, the work of Carl Zenker. Based on a bamboo airframe, it used four pairs of four-blade rotors for vertical lift and twin propellers to engage horizontal flight. Trials in 1900 proved the helicopter incapable of flight, but the layout was a precursor of those machines that followed a few years later which actually managed to lift from the ground.

Louis and Jacques Breguet, of the famed clockmaking family, and who were to found the world-famous Société des Avions Louis Breguet aeroplane manufacturing company in 1911, had begun with helicopters, designing with Professor Richet the *Gyroplane No 1*. This machine was huge and very basic, centred on a cruciform structure, with an eight-blade rotor at the apex of each boom, all powered by a single 50-hp Antoinette engine. Weighing 577 kg, the helicopter was intended only to prove the possibility of lifting its own weight and that of pilot-engineer Volumard, which it did in September 1907, at Douai, though it had to be steadied by four helpers with long poles. The first lift-off had managed just 0.6 m in the air, but on the 29th it raised to 1.5 m, and this is the flight that is recognised as having

been the first by a helicopter with a man on board.

Armed with this limited, but notable success, the Breguet brothers and Richet produced the large *Gyroplane No 2bis*, much more a hybrid between an aeroplane and a helicopter, with two sets of *No 1*-type rotors set at 40 degrees from the horizontal between biplane wings, and with a full set of aeroplane tail surfaces. Flown on 22 July 1908, it reached a 4-m height but was damaged on landing. This marked the culmination of their helicopter work, their next aircraft being a full aeroplane.

Meanwhile, French mechanic Paul Cornu had tested a model helicopter with a 2-hp Buchet engine, and it was upon this model that he designed and built a full-size, workmanlike 260-kg machine centred on a 24-hp Antoinette engine. Two rotors, each with two wide-chord

above
Paul Cornu sitting astride his successful free-flying helicopter of 1907. When his brother was left hanging onto the machine during the second flight, he reluctantly became the world's first passenger on a powered aircraft of any type.

blades mounted on a 1.77 m-diameter circular hub, were joined by fore and aft elevator surfaces that, when caught in the downwash from the rotors, could be controlled to adjust the helicopter's speed and direction.

On 13 November 1907, at Lisieux, the helicopter lifted Cornu off the ground for 20 glorious seconds, unaided, and to a height of 0.3 m. A free flight had now been made by a helicopter, although Cornu had taken the precaution of fixing a tethering line should it rise too quickly, which had no bearing on the flight. During the next attempt the helicopter rose so quickly to 1.5 m that Cornu's brother was left hanging on to the airframe. This little-known and often unrecorded event effectively made this the first two-man helicopter flight in history and made the brother the world's first powered aircraft passenger (of sorts) – ahead of Charles Furnas on a Wright biplane in May 1908! Other tests followed, but Cornu lacked the finances to continue to even greater achievements.

In 1912 Jacob Ellehammer (see p. 72) produced a 36-hp helicopter which lifted to about 0.6 m. Each of the two contra-rotating rotors had four blades attached to circular structures, the bottom rotor structure being covered to act also as a type of parachute. The importance of this helicopter was that it had a basic form of cyclic pitch control, whereby the blades advancing into the airstream adopted a shallow angle of pitch and the retreating blades adopted maximum pitch angle, thus creating even lift throughout the 360-degree rotor cycle. This was a vital discovery for helicopter development.

By World War I helicopters had contributed nothing to the general aviation scene, having made only the most tentative flights for very brief periods. However, during that war something quite remarkable took place, that is so often forgotten. Oberstleutnant Stefan von Petroczy of the Austrian Army Balloon

below

This truly remarkable and rare photograph shows a Petroczy-type helicopter during lifting trials in 1916. The ability of his helicopters to fly successfully with heavy loads and for long periods of time should be seen historically as equivalent to the technical lead established by the Wright brothers in the field of aeroplanes a decade earlier.

Corps followed his model helicopter experiments by having two full-size helicopters constructed, intended for trials as tethered military observation machines. The first, with an electric motor generating the equivalent of 190 hp, managed to lift three crew but burned out after running for 30 minutes. The second was powered by three 120-hp Le Rhône internal combustion engines that drove 6 m-diameter contra-rotating rotors mounted below a central cylindrical cockpit for the observer and gunner, the whole machine being winched out with rotors turning. A safety parachute could be deployed by the aircrew, or would deploy automatically if rotor rpm dropped to an unsafe level.

In trials, Petroczy's second helicopter proved capable of staying airborne for an hour, reaching 50-m altitude while tethered, and remained stable in 17-knot winds. Its lifting power far exceeded the weight of the two crew. After 14 successful flights, and with the engines by then requiring attention, an additional test was ordered, during which engine problems caused the crew to jump out by parachute and the helicopter was wrecked. So ended a series of truly remarkable trials.

In March 1918 Dr Ing Theodor von Kármán and Wilhelm Zurovec completed a new development of Petroczy's helicopter at Budapest, known as the PKZ 1. Using electric power to drive four rotors, it is thought to have made four flights, on three occasions carrying a crew of three. It was now Wilhelm Zurovec's turn to take the lead, and in April 1918 he demonstrated a new helicopter based very much on Petroczy's second machine. This too flew well in tethered form. However, nothing further came of these experiments, leaving others to take up the reins of vertical flight experimentation after peace returned to the world.

The First Air Wars

THE IMAGE OF 'STICK AND STRING' BIPLANES LUMBERING INTO THE SKIES FOR ARTILLERY SPOTTING AND RECONNAISSANCE IN THE EARLY DAYS OF WORLD WAR I can easily give the misleading impression that this was the first air war. Far from it. The benefits derived from having an eye in the sky were understood by military planners at the very outset of manned flying.

The French Revolution, that stifled scientific advance for a brief period in that country, just as suddenly became the instrument of progress in order to prepare aeronautics for warfare. In 1793 the French Aerostatic Corps was created in secrecy at Meudon, comprising a single tethered hydrogen balloon for observation training and 50 recruits under direction of Capitaine Coutelle.

About that time a vast French army was in battle with the Austrians and Dutch over the Southern Netherlands (Belgium). To see whether the Aerostatic Corps could assist General Jourdan's forces, the Committee of Public Safety sent Coutelle to Beaumont where, on arrival, the Commissioner of the Convention threatened to have him shot as a spy! Fortunately, all was explained and Coutelle was further dispatched to Maubeuge to observe the opposing forces.

Having returned home and experimented with a balloon better suited to the task, and having worked out methods of signalling to the ground, Coutelle – now Brevet-Capitaine of the Aerostatic Corps of the Artillery Service – returned to Maubeuge. There he established camp and set up the new hydrogen kiln, while awaiting arrival of the balloon *Entreprenant*. On 26 June 1794, during the Battle of Fleurus, Coutelle and another officer flew two separate four-hour tethered observation missions. These were the first-ever manned air missions in warfare, and the first time a manned aircraft had been on the receiving end of rifle and cannon groundfire. Before long other 'operational' balloons had been accepted into service, including one balloon for each of the French Republican armies of the Rhine and Moselle, Sambre and Meuse, and Egypt, with the army of the North keeping *Entreprenant*.

Amazingly, Napoleon Bonaparte disbanded the Aerostatic Corps in 1799, probably because he found the equipment slowed him down during the Egyptian campaign, when the army of Egypt's balloon *Intrépide* and its equipment finished at the bottom of Aboukir Bay after a naval engagement. Nevertheless, military ballooning in France had not ended for good. Indeed, as the twentieth century dawned the French army used tethered balloons in Morocco (1907), and observation balloons became commonplace to many combatant nations in World War I.

It seems incongruous that balloons could ever have become a strategic offensive weapon, but this is exactly what happened for the first time on 22 August 1849, when Austria launched unmanned balloons against Venice, each armed with a 14-kg bomb that was to explode via a time fuse. This tactic was again used by the Japanese in World War II, from November 1944, when it launched some 9,000 unmanned balloons to fly the Pacific Ocean and attack the USA, a journey of nearly 10,000 km. Each Japanese balloon carried a constant-altitude device to make full use of the prevailing jet stream, and a 15-kg anti-personnel bomb and two incendiary bombs. It is believed that some 1,000 actually reached the USA. However, as with the Austrian bomb-balloons a century before, they failed to demoralise the public and caused only a tiny number of casualties.

THE AMERICAN CIVIL WAR became the backdrop for the first US air force of sorts, founded on 1 October 1861 as part of the Army of the Union. Thaddeus Sobieski Constantine Lowe – who, on 18 June that year, had flown the balloon *Enterprise* from which was sent the first telegraph message ever to be transmitted from the air (passed on to President Lincoln) – was appointed Chief Aeronaut to General McClellan's Balloon Corps, Army of the Potomac, having a complement of 50 men.

Although disbanded in 1863, the Corps' seven balloons conducted a great deal of very useful work in the field of observation and artillery directing, benefiting from a simple and mobile

Austrian unmanned balloons float over Venice in 1849, each carrying a 14-kg bomb with time fuse. Little damage was caused in this first-ever balloon bombing raid.

left
Thaddeus Lowe
conducted a great deal of
useful work from
balloons during the
American Civil War,
observing Confederate
forces and directing
artillery. Here Lowe
ascends (tethered) at Fair
Oaks on 31 May 1862.
He also made free flights
when advantageous.

system of hydrogen gas production that adopted a new process using dilute sulphuric acid reacting with iron and purified by lime. Almost from the outset, the Corps had used the converted coal barge *George Washington Parke Custis* for both transportation along the Potomac River and as a tethering platform from which to observe Confederate forces, thereby becoming by definition the world's first aircraft carrier.

Interestingly, the first-ever American to be shot down by enemy action was also a balloonist, in 1898. As America and Spain fought over Cuba, Sergeant Ivy Baldwin of the US Army Signal Corps put forward the idea of observing Spanish forces from the air by balloon. During the Battle of Santiago, Baldwin managed to provide a good deal of information, which brought upon him Spanish groundfire that punctured the envelope. Fortunately, he fell into water with only slight injury to himself.

IMPORTANT TO MILITARY AVIATION IN EUROPE WAS THE FOUNDING, IN 1870, OF LIGHTER-THAN-AIR DETACHMENTS WITHIN THE PRUSSIAN ARMY. Assisted in their creation by Englishman Henry Coxwell, two Luftschiffer (airship) detachments were used immediately for service during the Franco–Prussian War of 1870–71. However, it was the defenders of besieged Paris that history most remembers.

above

Inflation of hydrogen balloons in the Place Saint Pierre in Montmartre during the Paris Commune operations of 1870–71. Three captive balloon sites had been established for reconnaissance during the siege of Paris, Franco-Prussian War, this being one. The famed aeronaut and photographer, M. Nadar Snr, conducted aerial observations and reconnaissance photography from this area. However, when the city was surrounded it became necessary to make free-flights out of the city to keep in touch with the provisional government

Cut off from outside help by Prussian forces, the Parisians made use of six balloons held within the city to fly out despatches, often under groundfire, the first by Jules Durouf on 23 September 1870 rising over Prussian lines and on to Evreux. Thereafter, a truly remarkable manufacturing programme was started in Paris, using railway stations and other large buildings to assemble additional craft, with gas coming from the Villette works. By 28 January 1871 a total of 66 balloons had left the city, carrying more than one hundred persons, some three million letters and carrier pigeons. Of these, two are thought to have been hit by groundfire from Prussian guns and seven drifted in the wrong direction. The escape of pigeons had been a vital element of the operation, as chemist Barreswil invented microphotography in October 1870 to allow the birds to return to Paris carrying messages, with the first flying from Tours to Paris on 18 November.

THE BRITISH ARMY FIRST DEPLOYED A MAN-CARRYING BALLOON during manoeuvres at Aldershot on 24 June 1880, and balloon detachments went with expeditionary forces to Mafeking in Bechuanaland in late 1884 and the Sudan in early 1885.

right
Military observation
balloon at Ladysmith,
South Africa.

above
Eugene B Ely, a civilian
pilot who proved that
military aircraft carriers
were possible.

A REAL BREAKTHROUGH IN AIR OBSERVATION came with the invention of the kite-balloon, or *Drachen*, by German officer August von Parseval and Bartsch von Sigsfeld. It was first deployed in manoeuvres by the German Army in 1897, its special shape offering increased stability in tethered flight. Its importance really came to light during World War I. Von Parseval also designed airships, 27 of which were built between 1906 and 1917, several for military service in Germany but with a few exported (including to Italy, Russia, Austria, Turkey and Japan), one even going to the Royal Navy as British Naval Airship No 4 in 1913; a second airship, ordered by Great Britain and launched in 1914, was taken over by the German Army and then handed over to the German Navy, but was destroyed at sea after a bombing raid in 1915.

Tethered balloons were also used with considerable success by Japan during its 1904–05 campaigns in Manchuria, by the Bulgarians in the Balkans, and by the Italians in 1911–12 during their war with Turkey over the disputed territories of Tripolitania and Cyrenaica in North Africa. The Italian campaign in Libya proved highly significant to the advent of air power, with the Air Flotilla also deploying *Drachen* kite-balloons, two airships of SCA semi-rigid type, and aeroplanes, as will be detailed later.

ALTHOUGH WRIGHT MODEL A *MISS COLUMBIA* HAD BECOME THE FIRST MILITARY AEROPLANE FOR SERVICE WITH THE US ARMY (on 2 August 1909 it was officially accepted at the staggering purchase price of $30,000), an Aeronautical Division of the Chief Signal Officer had already been established since August 1907. The Wright machine remained the Division's lone aeroplane for two years, and only with the financial provisions of Congress's 1912 budget could other machines be ordered, leading to the establishment of the 1st Aero Squadron in Texas in 1913.

Interestingly, two US Navy observers had been present at the US Army trials of the Wright biplane at Fort Myer in 1908, and had been keen to propose the idea of naval flying. But the Navy was not yet ready for such a radical move. What changed this view was an unrelated flight by Lt Paul Beck, on 19 January 1910, during which he dropped sandbags over Los Angeles from an aeroplane piloted by Louis Paulhan, so demonstrating aerial bombing as a formidable asset, or danger in warfare. This event so convinced the New York *World* newspaper that air power was the future of warfare, that it sponsored a further demonstration on 30 June, in which Glenn Curtiss undertook a mock bombing attack on the outline of a battleship, set out on Lake Keuka. From an altitude of 15 m, he dropped lead pipes to represent bombs.

Now ready to embrace at least the founding ideas of naval air power, in September 1910 the US Navy

seconded Captain Washington Irving Chambers to oversee naval aviation matters. The first step was to assess the problems associated with carrying aeroplanes or airships on board new scouting ships, but the Secretary of the Navy did not then authorise purchase of any aeroplanes. Once again fate took a hand in the form of the *World* newspaper. In league with the Hamburg–American Steamship Line, the newspaper made plans to fly an aeroplane off an ocean liner for mail delivery experiments. Not wanting the Navy to be beaten by civilians to the honour of flying from a ship, Chambers hurriedly obtained the use of USS *Birmingham* as a rival launch platform. To attempt the actual flight, Chambers acquired the services of civilian pilot Eugene Ely, a Curtiss company employee, who would use the Curtiss biplane *Hudson Flier*. Interestingly, the same aeroplane had already been used to win the $10,000 prize from the *World* newspaper for a flight between Albany and New York.

A series of delays for the civilian attempt allowed the Navy the chance to be first, a 25.3-m long and 7.3-m wide sloping wooden platform being built quickly over the bow of the cruiser. On 14 November 1910, impatient to get on with the flight after poor weather had prevented the cruiser from sailing, Ely decided to risk the flight without further postponement. Although the lack of headwind meant that he dropped towards the water after leaving the platform, damaging the propeller, he successfully recovered and flew to the nearest land.

While subsequent preparations were made to attempt an all-important landing on ship – the USS *Pennsylvania*, this time with a 36.36-m long and 9.6-m wide platform over the stern – on 26 January 1911

below
Ely lands on the 13,680 ton armoured cruiser,
USS *Pennsylvania*, anchored in San Francisco Bay. The 36-m
long wooden platform over the stern shows the rope and
sandbag arresting system to slow Ely's aeroplane to a halt.
'This is the most important landing of a bird since the dove
flew back to the Ark,' remarked Captain Pond.

Glenn Curtiss showed the potential of his company's aircraft in hydroaeroplane (seaplane) form by alighting on water, taxiing, taking-off and then alighting again. Then followed the successful landing on *Pennsylvania*, on 18 January 1911, when Ely's new Curtiss Model D-IV biplane came to rest after being slowed to a halt by a rope and sandbag arresting system placed on deck. The aircraft carrier was a reality, reinforced when, after eating with the crew, Ely took off again from the deck. Sadly, Ely died later that year in an aeroplane accident. On 17 February Glenn Curtiss taxied his seaplane to the *Pennsylvania*, which lifted man and machine on board and then returned both to the water for a return flight to land, a further boost to the concept of naval aviation.

After such exciting demonstrations, it took only until March 1911 for Congress to award $25,000 for further naval work, sufficient also to allow for the actual purchase for the Navy of two Curtiss aeroplanes and one Wright. The first of these flew in July 1911, as the Curtiss A-1 Triad, and it was this aircraft that Lt Theodore Ellyson used, on 31 July 1912, for the first catapult experiments using compressed air which, on this occasion, were not entirely successful, but later proved so.

Despite its slow start compared to the US Army, it was to be the Navy that undertook the first-ever military operations involving US aeroplanes. These took place from 25 April 1914, when five Curtiss AB flying-boats and seven pilots flew mine-countermeasures, reconnaissance and photographic missions during the Vera Cruz incident in Mexico, having been deployed in two detachments on board USS *Mississippi* and USS *Birmingham*.

BY 1909 OTHER NATIONS HAD ALSO BEGUN GEARING UP FOR MILITARY AEROPLANE FLYING. In France, the pending application of air power became a bitter struggle between the French Artillery and the Engineers, both of which initially fielded aeroplanes. This was resolved in April 1910 by the establishment of the Service Aéronautique as a section of the Army under the control of the Engineers, itself becoming the Aéronautique Militaire in October. Meanwhile, on 9 June 1910 Lt Féquant and Capitaine Marconnet undertook the first French reconnaissance mission by aeroplane, flying a Henry Farman biplane between Châlons and Vincennes. The next day the service received a Wright biplane.

By the September 1910 manoeuvres in Picardy, no fewer than 14 military aeroplanes were fielded by France, alongside four airships, with civil reserve pilots flying with regular military pilots. By the beginning of 1911 the French had 29 aeroplanes and 39 military pilots, leading to an important competition for new military aeroplane designs and a further expansion of airfields. Meanwhile, the French Navy had purchased its first aeroplane and assigned its first pilots in late 1910, with a seaplane following in 1911, and it established a new headquarters at Saint Raphael.

MILITARY EXPERIMENTATION WITH AEROPLANES AND THEIR INITIAL DEPLOYMENTS, and the actual founding dates for air forces as independent branches of a nation's overall military forces, often happened at entirely different times, which has created a haze over the true chronology of events. For example, the first official aeroplane flight in Great Britain was made on 16 October 1908 by the *British Army Aeroplane No 1*, a huge biplane designed by American-born (subsequently a naturalised British citizen) Samuel Franklin Cody for the British War Office, which Cody flew at Laffan's Plain in Farnborough over a distance of 424 m before

above

Britain was slow to take up aviation, and when the *British Army Aeroplane No 1* made the first officially recognised aeroplane flight in Great Britain, in October 1908, it was flown by American-born designer, Samuel Franklin Cody. Previously at Farnborough, Cody had conducted trials with man-carrying observation kites, starting in 1899.

crash landing. The same aeroplane and pilot became the first to fly for more than one mile (1.6 km) in Great Britain, on 14 May 1909. In September 1910 the British Army made its first aeroplane reconnaissance flight during the Grand Autumn Manoeuvres, using a Bristol Boxkite, but it was not until 13 May 1912 that the Royal Flying Corps was officially formed out of the former Air Battalion of the Royal Engineers, equipped with two aeroplane and one airship/manned kite squadrons.

The Naval Wing of the Royal Flying Corps was also founded on 13 May 1912, with Cdr Charles Rumney Samson becoming officer commanding that October; Samson is remembered for many flying achievements, not least for having been the first Royal Navy pilot to fly an aeroplane from a ship – actually a Short biplane from HMS *Africa* in December 1911, although officially recorded as a Short S.38 from *Africa* on 10 January 1912 – and the first pilot in the world to fly from a ship that was underway, this time HMS *Hibernia* on 9 May 1912. In June 1912, a French Navy Voisin flew from the cruiser *La Foudre*.

Military aeroplane flying in Germany and Italy also began in 1909, with Russia forming the Imperial Russian Flying Corps in 1910, although the actual German Military Aviation Service and the Italian Battaglione Aviatori were created after reorganisation of assets in 1912. For the Italians fighting Turkey from September 1911 over the territories of Tripolitania and Cyrenaica, it was down to its nucleus Air Flotilla to provide air operations. The dispatched Expeditionary Force included seven French-built aeroplanes of various types and two Austrian Taubes, all with no fixed armament, while the airships and kite-balloons

left

Cdr Charles Samson
leaves HMS *Africa*, a
17,500-ton adapted
battleship moored in
Sheerness Harbour.

below
A rare photograph of air
action over the Western
Front, with a Taube
being chased by a French
Farman.

mentioned previously followed on. On 22 October 1911 Capitano Piazza flew
a Blériot on a one-hour reconnaissance of Turkish forces between Tripoli and
Azizia, the very first aeroplane mission in any war. A second mission that day
by the pilot of a Nieuport gave grave warning of their susceptibility to enemy
groundfire, returning to base with damage. Nevertheless, risks had to be taken,
and a reconnaissance on 25 October gave advance notice of a Turkish attack.
But luck had to run out eventually and on 13 March 1912 Lt Cannonière was
wounded during a mission.

As the days passed, so the usefulness of Italian warplanes increased, with
additional roles including directing army and naval gunfire. Then, on
1 November, a Taube monoplane was flown by Tenente Gavotti over Ain Zara
and Taguira Oasis, from which four 2-kg Cipelli grenades were dropped, with
significant effect. Now aeroplanes had, for the first time, become bombers,

below
Italian Capitano Piazza with a Blériot monoplane before
making his reconnaissance flight that marked the very first
use of an aeroplane in war, 22 October 1911. This Blériot
was one of seven French aeroplanes and two Austrian
Taubes, all unarmed, taken to war by the Italian Air
Flotilla.

while Italian airships subsequently added a 'heavy' bombing option and conducted 91 operational missions against Turkish targets and positions. A French-built Henry Farman biplane was used as the platform for the first air-launched torpedo in war, while in February 1912 Piazza himself undertook the first-ever photographic reconnaissance mission, over Suani-Beni Adem. Piazza is also remembered for flying the first night mission of the war, in early 1912.

Other conflicts involving Bulgaria, Romania, Serbia, Turkey and Mexico in 1912–13 also witnessed the use of aeroplanes. The Mexican revolution was particularly relevant, as foreign pilots helped the various opposing forces. A Frenchman named Didier Masson, who supported General Alvarado Obregon, bombed gunboats in Guaymas Bay on 10 May 1913, while in November that year Phillip Rader, flying for General Huerta, and Dean Lamb supporting Venustiano Carranza, exchanged hand-gun fire during the world's first air-to-air combat. Similarly, French aeroplanes dropped bombs during the colonial campaign in Morocco, in which Capitaine Hervé and his observer Roëland became the first French air losses on active service, in early 1914, when they were fired on by tribesmen and were killed after making a forced landing in the desert.

THE FIRST AEROPLANE LOSSES TO GROUND FIRE were tragic, but hardly the result of effective anti-aircraft measures. Yet, even before these losses, the usefulness of aeroplanes over the battlefield and beyond had been so obvious that steps to ensure destruction of the enemy's machines became a separate priority. As early as 1910 the French demonstrated a motorcar with an upward-elevated machine-gun over the rear seats, while by 1911 the German Army fielded a much more effective mobile anti-aircraft cannon mounted on a specially modified truck. This was just the beginning.

Strangely, given early signs of limited success, arming aeroplanes themselves in a meaningful way took a very long time, and it is true to say that the majority of the world's military aircraft at the advent of World War I were unarmed and unsuitable to be armed. Yet, it was not for the lack of forethought. Even before Lt Jacob Fickel of the US Army fired a rifle from a two-seat Curtiss biplane on 20 August 1910, August Euler (incidentally, the first German to receive a pilot's licence) had been granted, on 24 July 1910, a patent for a mounting device that allowed a fixed machine-gun to be fired from an aeroplane, which he subsequently fitted to his *Gelber Hund* biplane. In Britain, Major Brooke-Popham got into very hot water with his superiors for attaching a gun to a Blériot.

Elsewhere, a rearward-firing machine-gun was neatly mounted on a French two-seat Nieuport monoplane for trials in 1911, and on 2 June 1912 a US Army Wright Model B two-seater was flown with Captain Charles de Forest Chandler manning a Lewis gun in a far less sophisticated set-up, which raised little interest and was promptly removed.

Meanwhile, on 7 January 1911 Americans Lt Myron Crissy and Philip Parmalee had dropped live bombs during demonstrations of air power at San Francisco, California, while in 1912 US trials began to assess the potential of aeroplanes for anti-submarine warfare, under the direction of Lt John Towers. In France an underwing bomb-launching system was shown by Lt Bousquet at Châlons in 1912, and at the Olympia Aero Show in Britain in early 1913 the Vickers EFB1 Destroyer was displayed, having been ordered by the Admiralty in 1912 as an experimental fighting aeroplane mounting a Maxim machine-gun. The Russian Dux-1 also appeared in 1913. Like the Destroyer, it was a pusher-engined biplane with forward-mounted gun.

bottom

One of the highlights of the 1913 Olympia Aero Show was the experimental Vickers EFB1 Destroyer, the first British aeroplane to be designed and built from the outset as an armed fighting machine, as ordered by the Admiralty. The Vickers-Maxim machine-gun could be aimed within 60 degrees of the vertical and horizontal. It is thought that the aircraft might have crashed on its first flight, but led to the FB5 Gunbus operational fighting scout. Also to be seen at the show was the Grahame-White Type 6, another armed aeroplane, but of more unusual design, with a Colt gun.

Whilst pusher-engined aeroplanes, or those front-engined types with tandem seats that allowed a rear gunner to fire away from the propeller, appeared to offer the best layout for arming, a more progressive approach had not been entirely overlooked. Frenchman Raymond Saulnier had experimented with a synchronising device that allowed machine-gun bullets to pass safely through the arc of a turning propeller without damaging the blades, intended to allow the pilot to line up a target and aim with the whole aeroplane, a particularly important step for single-seaters. However, his system relied on the propeller turning at a constant speed, which made it impractical. Similar work in Germany, by Franz Schneider, led him in July 1913 to patent a system that could operate at varying propeller speeds (see p. 109).

THE MARCH TO WORLD WAR began on 28 June 1914, when Archduke Franz Ferdinand, heir to the Austria–Hungary empire, was assassinated in Sarajevo. The resulting ultimatum from Austria–Hungary to Serbia on 23 July, that effectively demanded peace terms that transgressed Serbia's sovereignty, was accepted, but caused Russia to begin mobilisation. Germany in turn took this as an opportunity to mobilise its own forces, already having had the Schlieffen Plan in place since 1905 to subjugate both Russia and France, while France also had a plan which called for a quick strike north into Germany in case of war. On 1 August Germany declared war on Russia, while the next day its forces poured into Luxembourg as the first step in its plan to attack France via Belgium, declaring war on France on 3 August and marching into Belgium that day. Belgium, which had refused the German Army passage, had fewer than 20 aeroplanes with which to conduct reconnaissance flights against the invaders, and many of these were lost very quickly, but Belgium supplemented its depleted forces by taking over civil aircraft and purchasing extra French Farmans. Meanwhile, on 4 August, Great Britain had declared war on Germany, after Germany refused to guarantee Belgium neutrality. Like falling dominoes, other nations were to join the fray over the coming days .

The 1914–18 war was a defining point in history, quickly ending the old values and ways of nineteenth-century warfare, when cavalry charges by men in bright uniforms won or lost battles, replacing them after a few early skirmishes in 1914 with a rush to modern machines and towards indiscriminate destruction along battle lines that stretched across whole nations.

At the outset of war, the German Military Aviation Service had an inventory strength of 246 aeroplanes and seven large rigid airships, while the Imperial Naval Air Service added a further 36 aeroplanes and a large airship. The airships were of particular value due to their long range and good carrying

below
Von Zeppelin had LZ4 constructed as a long-range patrol airship for the German Army to demonstrate a 700 km day and night capability. Completed in mid-1908, it set out on a demonstration flight to Switzerland that July. The flight, already made eventful by engine problems, ended when the giant airship ripped loose in a storm while more engine repairs were underway on the ground, causing it to fall to earth as a damp and partially burned wreck.

above
The vulnerability of hydrogen-filled airships to destruction from enemy action or the elements is well demonstrated in this view of British officers inspecting the wrecked remains of a German airship.

capability, and before the year was out a further five Zeppelins had flown.

For Britain in 1914, the Royal Flying Corps (RFC) could in theory call upon 179 aircraft and the Royal Naval Air Service (RNAS) – formed in July 1914 from the former Naval Wing of the RFC – a further 78, numbers which included some non-rigid airships. To the allies, the French Aviation Militaire could contribute 160 aeroplanes and 15 airships, while French naval aviation had yet to improve upon eight machines. The Imperial Russian Air Service fielded mostly French-designed aeroplanes, numbering 244, while its naval equivalent had some water-borne machines. Austria–Hungary, as Germany's main ally, had 36 aeroplanes and a non-rigid airship.

These figures were, however, paper strengths and included outmoded training machines and others unfit for the air, and the actual number of suitable aircraft immediately available for front-line duty was vastly fewer. RFC aircraft first landed in France on 13 August 1914, and within a short time 73 machines provided the initial force, mostly suited to observation, reconnaissance and artillery co-operation work. By then both the RFC and German Military Aviation Service had already lost their first pilots to crashes.

FOR THE ALLIES, IT WAS THE POTENTIAL DESTRUCTIVE POWER and long reconnaissance range of the huge German rigid airships that conditioned the selection of the first targets to be bombed, although the aeroplanes to carry out such raids were barely up to the task. Nevertheless, on 14 August 1914 French Lt Césari and Corporal Prudhommeau, crewing a single aeroplane, raided the Zeppelin sheds at Metz-Frescaty, marking the very first bombing attack of the war.

The RNAS, which was fundamentally a home-defence organisation, opened its own campaign in August 1914 by making reconnaissance flights around the Belgium coast in support of the Royal Marines, led by Wg Cdr Charles Samson of the Eastchurch Squadron, which became the first RNAS squadron in France. With no permanently armed aircraft at all except for the Astra-Torres airship No 3, the Eastchurch Squadron nevertheless made a huge impact on early fighting. On 22 September 1914 four of its aircraft set out to make the first British air raids on Germany, targeting the airship sheds at Düsseldorf and Cologne. Only Flt Lt Collet found the target, at Düsseldorf, but none of the three 9-kg Hales bombs he carried exploded. A second raid on the same targets by the squadron, on 8 October, saw two Sopwith Tabloids head out from Antwerp, successfully destroying Zeppelin LZ25/Z.IX and its shed at Düsseldorf, while the railway station at Cologne was also bombed, marking the first successful British bombing raid of the war.

It is interesting to note here that the Tabloid is remembered also for being the first single-seat scouting aeroplane in the world to enter production for military service, having first flown in late 1913, although the

above

Designed as a pre-war two-seater, the Sopwith Tabloid went into military production as a single-seater, its 100 horsepower Gnome Monsoupape rotary engine giving this little biplane a very useful 148 km/h top speed. Unable to be adequately armed for air-to-air fighting, it nevertheless excelled in the early months of World War I as a scout and light bomber, including taking part in an historic raid against German airship sites.

provision of a wing-mounted machine-gun for Eastchurch Squadron aircraft did not take place until February 1915. On 21 November 1914 three RNAS Avro 504s operating out of Belfort, France, made the world's first formation strategic attack, damaging Zeppelin LZ32/L7 in its shed at Friedrichshafen and destroying the associated gasworks.

GERMAN RIGID AIRSHIPS were deployed by both the German Army and Navy, the latter becoming by far the greatest and most important operator. Military airships comprised not only the famed Zeppelins, but also the less plentiful Schütte-Lanz types. The first Schütte-Lanz had appeared in 1911, as the SL1, the first rigid airship to employ a wooden structure. The German Army took SL1 and, in 1914, the larger SL2, the latter being regarded as the first of the modern-style rigids, having introduced cruciform tail surfaces with elevators and rudders, and an enclosed control car at the nose for the crew; SL2 was operated on both the Western and Eastern Fronts but was lost in a storm in 1916.

The third Schütte-Lanz was the SL3, launched in 1915 and the first to be used by the Navy (until it crashed in 1916). Of 17 Schütte-Lanz rigid airships used in World War I, five were wrecked or crashed, four were burned or exploded, one was lost over the Black Sea, one was shot down, and six were dismantled or decommissioned in 1917.

Similar mixed fates befell the Zeppelins. The first Zeppelin rigid airship for military use had been the LZ3, launched on 9 October 1906 and taken by the German Army as Z.I in June 1909. This was decommissioned in 1913. LZ4 was also purchased in 1909 by the Army, as Z.II, but was destroyed in 1910. LZ14, launched in 1912, became the first German Navy Zeppelin, as L1, but this too failed to see action in World War I,

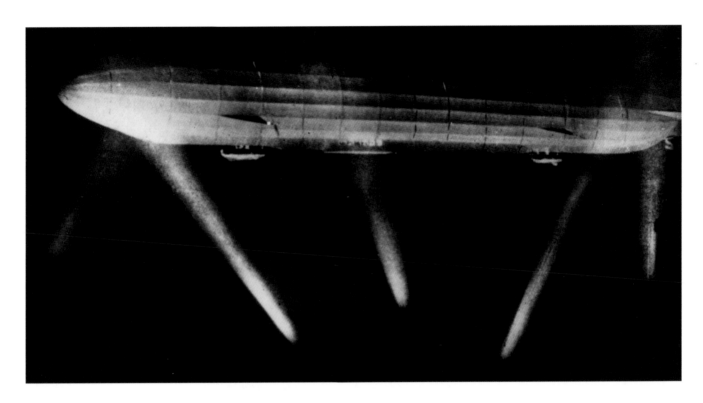

above

A German Zeppelin
airship on a strategic
bombing mission in 1916
is caught in the
defenders' searchlights.
Inadequate early
defences made the
interception of airships
extremely difficult, and
even when located poor
gunnery and the slow
climb rate of fighters
usually gave the raider a
high probability of
escape.

being lost over the North Sea during manoeuvres in 1913. However, the close ties between the Zeppelin and the German Navy had been established, strengthened in 1913 by Grand Admiral Alfred von Tirpitz's rapid expansion plans for ten airships in five years to equip two naval units, intended to make the Naval Airship Division by far the largest airship operator in the world.

The first of Tirpitz's new Zeppelins was launched in September 1913, as LZ18/L2. This was the first to be designed specifically to be capable of reaching Great Britain with a bomb load, should the need arise. At 158-m length and powered by four 165-horsepower Maybach engines, it was a giant for its day, but it caught fire while airborne on 17 October that year and all the 28 crew was lost.

Remarkably, the loss of two Zeppelins in close succession in 1913 did not deter the progress of giant airships into naval service. Indeed, by the Armistice in 1918, the Airship Division had operated 69 rigid airships of both types, making a huge number of sorties but in the process losing a great many of its number to the weather, crashes, accidents, enemy action and fire, with about 40 per cent of its personnel killed. Indeed, on 20 October 1917 the Airship Division lost no fewer than five Zeppelins in a single day, repeated on 5 January 1918 when five were caught in an explosion at the Ahlhorn sheds.

THE FIRST SUCCESSFUL GERMAN AIRSHIP MISSION OF WORLD WAR I took place on 12 August 1914, when the Naval Airship Division's new Zeppelin L3 located Dutch warships off Terschelling, Waddeneilanden. Three days earlier, the French Army non-rigid airship *Fleurus* had carried out the first Allied airship attack of the war, although this early success was tainted on 24 August when French infantry shot down its own airship Chalais-Meudon *Dupuy-de-Lôme*, believing it to be a Zeppelin.

German airship raids on Great Britain began on 19 January 1915, when two Naval Airship Division Zeppelins (a third having turned back because of engine problems) dropped bombs on Great Yarmouth,

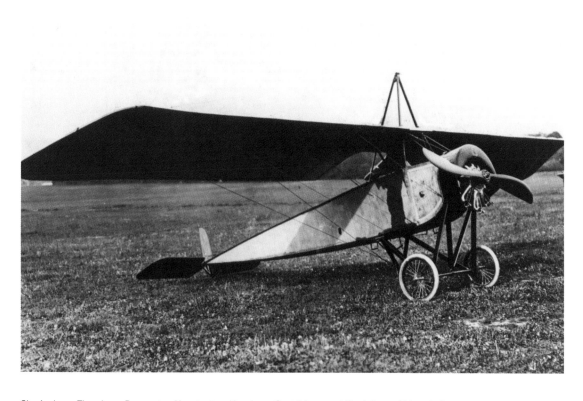

left

A French Morane-Saulnier Type L, of 1913 appearance. A standard machine in French service at the outbreak of World War I, it was initially unarmed, except for hand-guns carried by the crew or light bombs to be thrown overboard. Those exported included 25 delivered to the Royal Naval Air Service, allowing Warneford to claim a 'downed' Zeppelin in June 1915. Later attempts to arm the Type L included a machine-gun attached to the upper wing, to fire outside the propeller arc, but by 1916 the 114 km/h parasol-wing scout was completely outclassed and withdrawn.

Sheringham, Thornham, Brancaster, Hunstanton, Heacham, Snettisham and King's Lynn. Although the damage was not substantial and the number of those killed or injured was not great, it caused some panic among people who had never before had to consider air raids. The attack highlighted the need for proper home air defences. Both these Zeppelins were to be wrecked less than a month later, after a sortie to locate the British fleet.

On 3 May 1915, Zeppelin LZ36/L9 made the first partially successful attack on a submarine, when it damaged the conning tower of the Royal Navy D4 using 50-kg bombs. But May was to witness a far more sinister attack. On the night of the 31st, under the authority of the German Kaiser, Zeppelin LZ38 undertook the first air raid on London, the 1,360 kg of bombs dropped killing seven people and injuring 14 more.

Among the many difficulties in dealing with the German airship menace were the airship's virtually silent and high-altitude method of cruising, often undertaking night missions, its machine-gun defences, and a lack of suitable Allied aeroplanes with appropriate armament to carry out successful interceptions. Nevertheless, attacked they had to be!

On the night of 6/7 June 1915 three Zeppelins set out from Bruges to raid London, but bad weather forced them to abandon this and attack the Calais railways instead. One airship, the LZ37, was located by RNAS pilot R. A. J. Warneford of No 1 Squadron, who was flying a Morane-Saulnier Type L monoplane out of Dunkirk. With no machine-guns, he only had at his disposal six 9-kg Hales bombs. LZ37's gunners kept him at bay as he tracked the airship's progress from Ostend to Ghent. Then, in an incredibly bold move, he flew a single pass over the top, dropping all his bombs from 45 m overhead. The last exploded and LZ37 fell in flames, killing all the crew except for one. For this brave act he was awarded the Victoria Cross, but he lost his own life just 12 days later when the Henry Farman he was flying collapsed in mid-air.

Now that the first German giant had been dealt a fatal blow, others would eventually follow. Anti-aircraft

above

A 'downed' German Gotha GIV bomber being guarded by a British soldier at Margate. The giant Gotha GIV became operational in 1917, by which time it had become obvious that airships were no longer adequate as strategic raiders. Able to operate at 6,500 m altitude due to two excellent 260 horsepower Mercedes engines – although more usually 4,500 m – the Gothas of Bombengeschwader 3 alone averaged 3,835 kg of bombs during each of its 22 raids on England, massive attacks for the time. To counter the bomber threat, some fighters were withdrawn from France to defend the UK, with 1917 fighters of Sopwith Camel and Royal Aircraft Factory SE5 types finally having the pace to meet the challenge effectively. Yet, despite this, and after switching to night raids, by the end of the war more Gothas had been lost in operating accidents than to Allied action.

fire from the ground, combined with explosive darts dropped from an RFC BE2c biplane, brought down Zeppelin LZ48/L15 during a raid on England by five airships on the night of 31 March 1916, finishing in the sea and later sinking. This marked the first Zeppelin to be brought down over the British Isles, while on the night of 2 September 1916 Army airship Schütte-Lanz SL11 was the first to be brought down on British soil, when RFC pilot Lt W. Leefe Robinson set it on fire using the new Pomeroy incendiary ammunition. He too received the VC.

Despite these successes and others, German airship raids continued on Britain until 12 April 1918, when the last to cause injury to the British people took place. In all, Britain had withstood 51 such attacks, during which 199 tonnes of bombs had killed 557 people. But the destruction of SL11 in 1916 had greatly demoralised German airship crews and was thought to have prevented a planned large-scale raid on London.

HAVING COME TO GRIPS WITH THE AIRSHIP MENACE, ON 28 NOVEMBER 1916 LONDON BECAME THE TARGET FOR A GERMAN AEROPLANE ATTACK, although the small LVG CII biplane only carried six light bombs that fell near to Victoria Station. But mass bombing raids by German heavy bombers on England were only months away. On 25 May 1917, a total of 21 German Gotha heavy bombers attacked several towns, killing 95 and injuring 195 more. The difficulty of dealing with bombers was highlighted when none of the 77 sorties flown by defending aircraft made contact with the bombers. On 13 June London became the target of a mass raid, 14 German heavy bombers dropping 72 bombs in the Liverpool Street Station area, killing 162 and injuring 432 more. In terms of death and injury, this was the worst bombing raid of the war.

A major raid on England on 12 August 1917 was the last in daylight, as even the bombers were by then becoming susceptible to new well-planned defences. Mass night raids on England by Gothas began on 3 September 1917, with Dover the target. Then, two weeks later, the even larger German Staaken R VI bombers headed out to attack England, each capable of carrying a 1,000-kg punch. But, in January 1918, the RFC got its revenge, when two Sopwith Camel fighters of No 44 Squadron brought down a Gotha at night. By May even the night raids ceased.

ALLIED BOMBING AT THE START OF THE WAR had been light, with German airships and their sheds as important targets. On 30 August 1914 Paris had been bombed by the German pilot of a Taube monoplane, his five small bombs killing one woman and causing injury to two other people – in the early stages of the war, Taubes made many nuisance raids on Allied targets as the most prevalent warplane in German service. Not to be outdone, on 27 September 1914 France formed its first bomber group, although fairly lightly equipped with Voisin pusher biplanes.

Italy, once it joined the Allied cause by declaring war on Austria–Hungary on 24 May 1915, set about plans for a sustained strategic bombing offensive, which started during daylight hours on 20 August that year, using mainly Caproni Ca 32s. The same machines also opened Italy's night offensive.

On the Eastern Front, on 15 February 1915 Russia opened its heavy bomber offensive by raiding a target in Poland, using its giant four-engined Ilya Mourometz biplanes. Some 400 bombing raids were conducted by these bombers during the war, sometimes escorted by Sikorsky S-16 purpose-designed fighters.

below
A French Voisin 10 ground attack biplane, fitted with a
37-mm Hotchkiss cannon. This was the final version of
the so-called Voisin 'Chicken Coop', for service in 1918.
Other than its 300 horsepower Renault engine, 132 km/h
speed and 300-kg bomb-load, it actually differed little
from its 1914–17 ancestors.

**FOR THE FIRST BRITISH SQUADRON ESTABLISHED
SPECIFICALLY FOR NIGHT BOMBING, GERMAN FIGHTER
UNITS WERE ITS INITIAL TARGET.** No 100 Squadron,
RFC, had been formed in February 1917 and
reached France the following month, where it
eventually established its base at Le Hameau. To
open its score, on the night of 5/6 April its light
Royal Aircraft Factory FE2b biplanes made two
attacks on the airfield at Douai, home base of the
squadrons led by German fighter ace Rittmeister
Manfred Freiherr von Richthofen, the Red Baron.
These German squadrons had collectively
become known to the Allies as the 'Richthofen
Circus' because of their brightly painted aircraft.
In the attack, four hangars sustained heavy
damage, but one FE2b was lost.

On 11 October 1917, the RFC formed the 41st
Wing specifically to carry out strategic bombing
of German targets. Then, on 5 June 1918,
following the realignment on 1 April 1918 of the
RFC and RNAS into the new single Royal Air
Force, the RAF created the so-called Independent
Force under Major-General Sir Hugh Trenchard,
to conduct a major strategic offensive against
German industrial and military targets.
Meanwhile, back in 1916, the RFC had taken into
service the Handley Page O/100 heavy bomber,
designed as a 'bloody paralyser' as pay-back for
German raids. From the O/100 was developed the
improved O/400 which, in 1918, became standard
equipment with the Independent Force. For an
attack in September 1918, no fewer than 40
bombers were despatched against the area of
Saar, the largest single force ever up to that time.
Furthermore, both the O/100 and O/400 began
fielding the 1,650-lb (748-kg) 'block buster' bomb
about this time, a truly devastating weapon.

left
The Ace of Aces,
Rittmeister Manfred,
Freiherr von Richthofen,
the so-called Red Baron,
who became the most
successful fighter pilot of
World War I, with 80
recorded victories. Close
behind were British
Major Edward Mannock
with 73 and French
Capitaine René Fonck
with 75, although it is
known that Mannock
unselfishly 'gave away'
several shared victories
to other pilots.

Handley Page O/400 heavy bomber of 1918. Faster than its German Gotha counterpart, due to its twin 360 horsepower Rolls-Royce Eagle VIII engines providing the power to attain 157 km/h, and with nearly twice the available bomb load, it nevertheless had a much lower operating ceiling. About to go into service when the Armistice was signed was the even larger Handley Page V/1500, the RAF's first ever four-engined bomber, and the first designed to attack the strategic heart of an enemy from home bases, having a duration of 17 hours, more than twice that of the O/400.

ALTHOUGH THE FIRST FIGHTER-SCOUT AEROPLANES HAD BEEN DEVELOPED BEFORE THE OUTBREAK OF WAR, proper exploitation of fighters was triggered only when it was proved by events that aerial reconnaissance and aerial bombing were having a major effect on planning, on the outcome of battles and on the movement of men and materials to the Front, when a means had to be found to stop the enemy from carrying out its work. Thus, in consequence, fighters were required also as escorts to 'friendly' aircraft conducting similar work, and for home defence. The concept of achieving air dominance through wholesale air-to-air combat between fighters alone came later, leading to the epic dogfighting of the war.

In 1914, reconnaissance was viewed as the main duty of front-line warplanes and, indeed, only six days after landing in France at the start of the war a Royal Aircraft Factory BE2a and Blériot of No 4 Squadron undertook the historic first British reconnaissance mission over German territory. Interestingly, on 25 August 1914 the RFC gained its first 'air victory', when unarmed machines of No 2 Squadron forced an unarmed German two-seater to land.

The BE2, which had reconnaissance as its main role but was also employed for light bombing, was a masterpiece of design for its time, its inherent stability making it an ideal platform for these

The Royal Aircraft Factory BE2 prototype, with much more cut-away cockpit than found on actual production versions for service in World War I.

purposes. But this very quality, combined with its slow speed and lack of any defensive armament, also made the BE2 highly vulnerable to attack once the Germans fielded more armed aircraft and then purpose-designed fighters. Thus, by mid-1915 the early models were being withdrawn and replaced by the BE2c variant with defensive machine-gun armament, aerodynamic improvements and a more powerful engine. Unfortunately, mounting the gun in the forward cockpit made its field of fire very restricted. Despite becoming one of the principal victims of the 'Fokker (Eindecker fighter) Scourge' in the winter of 1915–16, various models of the BE2 continued in service throughout the war, taking another round of extremely harsh punishment at German hands in 'Bloody April' 1917.

Among the fairly few armed aeroplanes at the start of the war, on both sides, could be counted the French Voisin pusher biplane, although the Hotchkiss machine-gun on the 105-km/h Voisin was intended

above

130 km/h Fokker EII
Eindecker, a
strengthened version of
the initial EI, serving
from September 1915.
Its Spandau machine-
gun is clearly visible in
front of the cockpit,
slightly offset starboard.

mainly for defence while pressing home light bombing raids, and for ground-attack missions, but could also be turned against other aeroplanes. It was a Voisin of Escadrille VB24 that destroyed a German Aviatik two-seater on 5 October 1914, the very first aeroplane to be shot down by another.

Vickers, whose Destroyer EFB 1 had been ordered by the British Admiralty in 1912 as a one-off experimental armed fighting machine, had been quick to see the potential for a purpose-designed fighting warplane and had continued development along these lines. With its FB5 of 1914, it took the bold step of putting the first 50 machines into production as a company initiative. After acceptance trials in the summer of 1914, FB5s were ordered for the RFC and RNAS. The first aircraft reached the Western Front from February 1915 and the first squadrons were operational by the summer. But events would make this 113-km/h fighter obsolete by the end of the year.

The Voisin and FB5 were both pusher-engined two-seaters, which allowed the front crew member to operate the gun on a movable mounting and have a good field of fire. But new aircraft, whose purpose was specifically air-to-air fighting, did not require a second crew member, which meant that the gun was better mounted in a fixed position. For those wishing to mount a gun on a single-seater with a forward tractor engine, and at eye level for easy aiming, the design problems only increased.

In truth, the main problem in arming tractor-engined aeroplanes had already been solved by the

synchronising device of Franz Schneider (see p. 99). His 1913 patented system could operate at varying propeller speeds, a crucial factor in its success. A version of this was eventually fitted for operational trials to the experimental LVG E.VI two-seat monoplane in 1915. However, this aeroplane was lost while *en route* to the Western Front.

The first single-seat fighter to gain an air victory over an enemy aeroplane, having fired its machine-gun through the propeller arc, was not, however, German. As mentioned earlier, Frenchman Raymond Saulnier had experimented with his own synchronising device for guns before the war, but this was impractical for requiring a constant propeller speed. Like others, Saulnier had also considered a fixed gun firing outside the propeller arc, and numbers of Morane-Saulnier Type L parasol-wing monoplanes had appeared early in the war with wing-mounted guns. But, he still remained convinced of the need to have the gun at eye level, and so he devised the incredibly basic system of attaching wedges to the propeller. This allowed bursts of bullets to be fired through the arc of a turning propeller, with the wedges merely deflecting away any bullets that would otherwise have hit and damaged the blades. The first Morane-Saulnier Type N equipped with a gun and propeller wedges was handed over to Frenchman Roland Garros, who from 1 April 1915 quickly claimed several unsuspecting enemy aircraft, as did other French pilots in similar

above

Frenchman, Roland Garros, who flew the first aeroplane with armoured steel wedges attached to the propeller to allow a machine-gun to fire through the propeller arch without the need for an efficient gun-propeller synchronising mechanism to prevent damage. With the capture of his aircraft by the Germans, it was not the discovery of the wedges themselves that proved critical, but that the Germans realised the urgency to develop proper air fighting aeroplanes.

machines. Then, on 19 April, Garros was hit by enemy groundfire and was forced to land behind German lines, where his aeroplane was captured. His secret was out.

Although the Germans then also considered similar wedges, Anthony Fokker instead applied synchronising technology to a Fokker M 5K reconnaissance monoplane, which became the M 5KMG. On 1 July 1915 an M 5KMG flown by Leutnant Kurt Wintgens brought down a Morane-Saulnier. From the M 5KMG was developed the famed Fokker E type Eindecker single-seat fighters of 1915–16, which wreaked havoc on Allied aeroplanes, despite the relatively small number deployed. It was the first time one side had air superiority over the other.

below

To counter the Fokker Eindecker, Britain fielded its own purpose-built, single-seat fighter, the Airco DH2 designed by Geoffrey de Havilland. Fast, responsive and strong, with a forward-mounted fixed Lewis machine-gun, it helped the Allies overcome the Fokker 'scourge' of 1915–16, but was itself outdated by 1917. Here DH2s of No 32 Squadron prepare for a mission over the Western Front.

In desperate attempts to counter the Eindecker, Britain deployed the two-seat Royal Aircraft Factory FE2b fighter during the winter of 1915–16 and then the single-seat Airco DH2 in 1916, both pusher-engined as Britain had no operational synchronising technology at that stage. The DH2 was the RFC's first-ever single-seat fighter. These gradually restored the balance of air power over the Western Front, in company with various French Nieuport biplanes that carried guns above the upper wing to fire outside the propeller arc.

For the Germans, having enjoyed the huge benefits of air superiority over the Western Front, fighter development could not be allowed to stand still. In the autumn of 1916 they started deploying new Albatros D type fighters as replacements for both the Eindecker and Halberstadt D types, possessing speeds and rates of climb which outmatched the Allies once again and heralded a second period of German air supremacy.

Then, until the end of the war, it became 'cat and mouse' for control of the skies, as the Allies countered with such aircraft as the French Spad, Hanriot HD-1 and new Nieuport designs, and the British Bristol F2 Fighter two-seater, single-seat Royal Aircraft Factory SE5, Sopwith Pup and Camel. For Germany, then deploying new Pfalz and improved Albatros fighters, amongst others, the crowning glory to their fighter

production came in 1918 with the Fokker DVII, the best German fighter of the war. Indeed, such was the menace this fighter posed to the Allies that it was specifically named in the Armistice Agreement for total surrender to the Allies. Post-war, Anthony Fokker fled to the Netherlands, taking a number of DVIIs and components with him. There he set up a new company and put the DVII back into production, which served with the Royal Netherlands Air Force until the 1930s.

AT SEA, LARGE FLYING-BOATS such as the American Curtiss America, French FBA and British Felixstowe F2 flew anti-submarine and coastal-patrol duties with considerable success, while smaller craft included Italian Macchi M series flying-boat fighters and Austro–Hungarian Löhner patrol types. Germany and Austria–Hungary, on the whole, though, preferred seaplanes for patrol and as station defence fighters, while all sides used seaplanes as torpedo bombers. But it was none of these countries that first sank a warship from the air – on 16 September 1914, Japanese Farman biplanes operating from the *Wakamiya Maru*

right
HMS *Engadine* in 1916, with a Shorts Admiralty Type 184 seaplane on the stern. A Type 184 from this seaplane carrier spotted 13 German Navy warships gathering for the Battle of Jutland, in 1916, seen as a milestone in naval aviation history.

seaplane carrier destroyed a German torpedo boat off China using improvised bombs made from naval shells.

The Royal Navy's *Ark Royal*, launched in 1914, became the world's first naval vessel to be converted to carry aeroplanes while still under construction, first deploying seaplanes against the Turks in the Dardanelles in February 1915. Turkish ships fell victim to Royal Navy Short 184 seaplanes operated from HMS *Ben-My-Chree* in August 1915, and in May 1916 a seaplane from HMS *Engadine* became the first aeroplane used in a major fleet battle, when it spotted German warships during the Battle of Jutland. In another theatre of war, on 15 September 1916 an Austro–Hungarian Löhner flying-boat sank the French vessel *Foucault*, the first submarine to be sunk through aeroplane attack.

BRITAIN LED THE WAY IN THE DEVELOPMENT OF AIRCRAFT CARRIERS FOR THE OPERATION OF LANDPLANES (as opposed to seaplane carriers), with the reassignment of the light battle-cruiser HMS *Furious* in 1917. By deleting one of its two intended 427-mm guns, *Furious* was able to be given a flight deck and hangar on its forecastle. Thus able to accommodate six Sopwith Pup fighters and four seaplanes, it was used initially to develop aeroplane operating techniques.

Landing aeroplanes while a ship was under way was uncharted territory, and on 2 August 1917 Sqn Cdr E. H. Dunning managed to perform the first-ever such landing on board *Furious*, with deck crew rushing to help stop the Pup as it side-slipped on to the deck, by grabbing straps hanging from the fighter. Unfortunately, a second attempt to land, on 7 August, ended in tragedy: Dunning stalled the Pup as he tried to overshoot and was killed when he was blown over the side of the ship. Nevertheless, development continued and new methods of arresting aircraft on deck were subsequently devised. Interestingly, on 19 July 1918 RNAS Sopwith Camels from *Furious* attacked and destroyed two Zeppelins in their sheds at Tondern, although of the seven

above

HMS *Furious*, recognised as the world's first aircraft carrier for operating landplanes. Laid
down after the outbreak of war as a light battle-cruiser with two large guns, modification
of the design to the new role was authorised in 1917, with the loss of one gun and the
addition of a flight deck and hangar on its forecastle. Initial equipment was six Sopwith
Pup fighters and four seaplanes. Through refits, *Furious* became the longest-serving carrier
in the world, surviving World War II, and was finally scrapped in 1949.

below
Sqn Cdr Dunning finally proved the aircraft carrier a reality
by showing that an aeroplane could land on a moving ship.
Successfully side-slipping his Sopwith Pup fighter onto the deck
of HMS *Furious* during the first trial, he was tragically killed
during the second. But, as events proved, it was the landing
method, rather than the concept, that needed rethinking.

fighters that took part, one pilot drowned, three landed in Denmark and the others had to ditch by the carrier. *Furious* continued in service until being scrapped in 1949, becoming the longest-serving active carrier of the time.

HMS *Argus* became the first flush-deck carrier, when completed in 1918, having been laid down originally in 1914 as an ocean liner for Italy. With a deck length of 172 m, *Argus* could carry 20 aircraft. In October 1918, the ship became the first carrier ever to embark with a full squadron of torpedo-carrying landplanes (Sopwith Cuckoos).

BY THE ARMISTICE ON 11 NOVEMBER 1918, air power had grown out of all recognition. The early lumbering machines of 1914, with their crews holding bombs to throw overboard, had been replaced by bombers and fighters with proper armament and delivery methods; and they were capable of twice the speed of their forebears, due in part to greatly improved airframe designs, but more importantly through the development of far more powerful and reliable inline and rotary engines. Wartime production in Britain had been a staggering 47,873 aeroplanes and nearly 52,600 engines, and this from an industry that had struggled to build 7,137 aeroplanes during the entire period from mid-1915 to early 1917. For Germany, approximately one-third of its wartime production of about 48,000 aeroplanes survived the war. Yet, strangely, France built only 24,652 aeroplanes (but over 92,000 engines), from which it had not only satisfied its own requirements but had bolstered British production and had supplied large numbers of machines to other nations too. America, once in the war from 1917, took in many French and British aeroplanes, but its own contributions to air power had been restricted principally to Curtiss JN 'Jenny' trainers and America flying-boats. Austria–Hungary and Italy had also developed worthy aircraft-manufacturing bases, with the Italians producing some of the finest heavy bombers of the war for their own forces and for use by other Allies, but Russia had relied heavily on French and British aircraft to bolster its own limited production.

AND SO PEACE RETURNED, and aircraft, such as the huge Vickers Vimy bomber that had barely managed to get a toe-hold on the fighting Fronts before the Armistice, had to carve their names in the post-war world, through air power and epic long-distance flights. Against defeated Germany, the Allies began with a determination to muzzle any further offensive capabilities. The German Army was restricted to 100,000 career soldiers for 'defence', with no conscription permitted as it was feared Germany could secretly build up a reserve force. The Army was to have no General Staff. The Navy was allowed 24 capital warships and 16,500 personnel, plus 12 torpedo boats, but absolutely no submarines. But the heaviest axe fell on the flying services. Without exception, Germany was to have no Army or Naval air forces, and all aeroplanes, airships, aircraft engines and associated equipment had to be surrendered to the victorious Allies. All military air training was forbidden, and the design and production of civil and commercial aircraft was restricted by rules limiting engine power, and manufacturers were not allowed to receive any government subsidy.

Defeated and humbled, as a final gesture of provocation the German Navy scuttled several of its warships in full view of the Allies, while, on 23 June 1919, crews of the Naval Airship Division destroyed six of its Zeppelins at Nordholz, five days before the terms of the peace treaty were officially signed.

New Industries and
Old Enemies – 1919–39

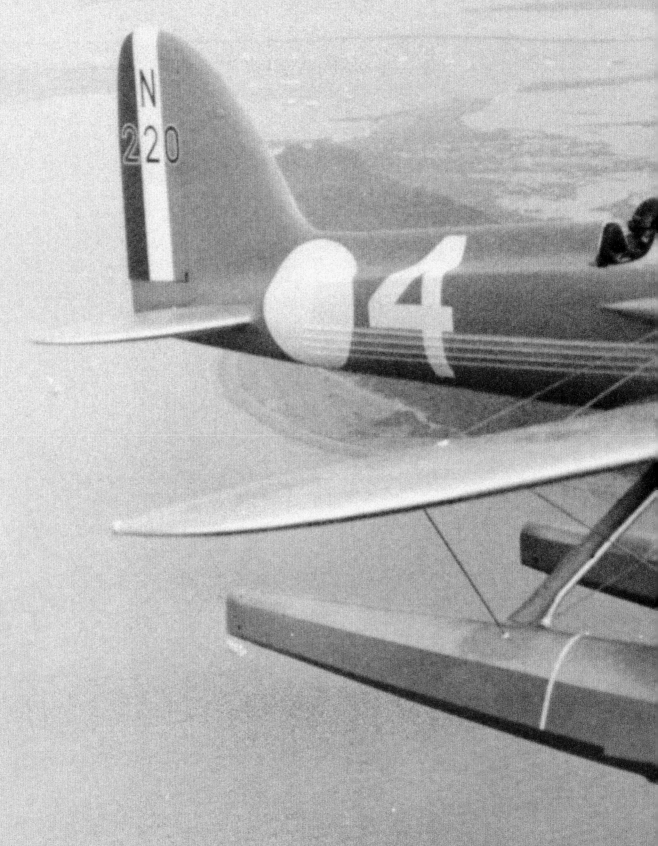

A TRAGEDY FOR EUROPE and European civilisation, the Great War of 1914–18 had, nevertheless, forced aircraft development to staggering new heights of achievement, but at dreadful cost. For many of the aircraft-manufacturing companies that had grown into vast concerns producing thousands of war-winning aeroplanes and aero-engines to government contracts, peace brought an unexpectedly sudden halt to much of their business. Whilst a few of the best new military aeroplanes would still be purchased for the immediate post-war era, the numbers were on the whole minimal as governments faced the task of having to decide what to do with so many unwanted operational aeroplanes and those still in their delivery crates.

Air forces quickly moved to peacetime levels, as huge economies were expected by cash-starved governments. The RAF, which had ended the war with 188 operational squadrons, was cut to just 12 squadrons by the end of 1919, plus a few naval air units. Indeed, it was only Britain's commitments to air operations over Iraq, India and Germany that kept the RAF alive, when just two squadrons remained at home.

One solution to the problem of unwanted aeroplanes was their sale at give-away prices, sometimes being used thereafter for the training of new civilian pilots, or for joy-riding, but also occasionally becoming stunt machines for barn-storming shows. Ex-military trainers were of particular use. The destruction of unwanted machines was another answer, or their sale abroad, while huge quantities of new engines that were not sold would sometimes be wrapped and stored or even buried. Some fledgling commercial airlines also found the inexpensive ex-military aeroplanes well suited to their early operations, ex-bombers occasionally receiving substantial modification but other smaller types justifying little expense towards passenger comfort. In the USA, the US Post Office purchased more than 125   ex-military aircraft, mainly of de Havilland DH4M type, with which to establish an airmail service between New York and San Francisco, realising that only a long-haul service could prove more economical and time-efficient over surface mail (see pages 122–123).

Newly designed commercial aeroplanes had to compete in this saturated market, until their comfort levels and economies made the cheap-alternative conversions untenable. Another new use for aeroplanes was created in 1921, when Huff Daland Dusters was founded at Monroe, USA, as the world's first aerial crop-dusting company, using aircraft of its own design.

The British Sopwith Aviation Company was a good example of how this turnabout production situation so greatly affected manufacturing companies; this company had produced such wartime masterpieces as the Triplane, Pup and Camel, but had only managed to get some 100 of its new Snipe fighters into service by the Armistice. However, having been proved in combat – not least when Major W. G. Barker won the Victoria Cross for his epic single-handed fight against 15 German Fokker DVIIs in the final days of the war – the Snipe became the RAF's first post-war standard fighter. A total of 497 was eventually produced by several companies, against wartime orders in 1918 that had envisaged 4,000. In 1920, having tried to bolster its business by producing motorcycles, the great Sopwith company went into liquidation.

Instances of manufacturers struggling to stay in business were many, and for a time it became necessary for them to rein back drastically while looking for new markets, or sink. Short Brothers, having lost its military seaplane work and with its final rigid airship nearing completion, began building boats and the bodies for omnibuses while still trying to develop new aeroplanes suited in small numbers to the post-war world. The latter included small sporting seaplanes and flying-boats, but its most successful entry back into manufacturing came with the development of long-range flying-boats, starting with the Singapore biplane.

Although the original Singapore prototype flew in 1926, the production Singapore III did not enter the RAF until the mid-1930s. However, the prototype was used for Alan Cobham's Round Africa flight of 1927–28 in civil markings, and this aircraft quickly led to the Calcutta commercial flying-boat derivative for Imperial Airways (Britain's first national airline, founded in 1924) and encouraged Shorts on to the much more modern and majestic C-Class flying-boat monoplanes, mostly for the same airline for use over its highly successful long-range Empire commercial routes in the 1930s.

The same problems faced foreign manufacturers. In France, having produced some 10,000 aircraft during the war, Voisin gave up in 1920 and turned to automobiles. Boeing in the USA survived this period of uncertainty mainly by constructing aeroplanes for other companies and building furniture and sea sled boats. And so it went on.

THE FIRST POST-WAR AIRLINES HAD ACTUALLY BEEN FOUNDED IN 1916-17, when the British Aircraft Transport & Travel Ltd (AT&T) and the German Deutsche Luft-Reederei (DLR) were registered. British civil flying remained prohibited until 1 May 1919, when the Air Navigation Regulations were published, which meant that from February until May AT&T could only operate humanitarian flights, carrying food and clothing, between Folkestone and Ghent in Belgium using converted Airco DH9 light bombers and RAF aircrew. The Farman brothers in France, meanwhile, got around the UK civil passenger ban by flying military passengers between Paris and London on board their F60 Goliath (a newly built commercial variant of the forthcoming night bomber), from 8 February, while on 22 March the Farman brothers began the first sustained international services for commercial passengers, operating between Paris and Brussels. DLR began flights between Berlin and Weimar in February 1919.

In Britain, London Airport was inaugurated in July 1919, allowing AT&T to begin daily flights between London and Paris from 25 August using the first British purpose-built airliner, the de Havilland DH16, thereby founding the world's first scheduled international aeroplane service. Simultaneously, airlines were beginning to appear all over the world. After the Royal Dutch airline, KLM, had been formed in October 1919, co-operation with AT&T allowed an Amsterdam–London service from May 1920.

AT&T flew its last commercial service in December 1920 and was succeeded by Daimler Airway which, on 7 April 1922, saw one of its de Havilland DH18 airliners collide with a Grands Express Aériens Goliath over Thieuloy-Saint-Antoine in France, registering the world's first air collision between airliners on scheduled services. In 1924 Daimler Airway and three other British airlines merged to form Imperial Airways. National airlines were also forming elsewhere about this time, including Dobrolet in the Soviet Union and Sabena in Belgium, both in 1923.

In Germany, with its air industry greatly restricted by the terms of the Versailles Treaty, a national airline was created in 1926 as Deutsche Luft-Hansa (DLH), by the merger of Deutscher Aero Lloyd and Junkers Luftverkehr. The Junkers airline had been formed in 1921 by the aircraft manufacturer Junkers Flugzeugwerke as a means of promoting its own products, while its willingness to help establish airlines in various continents meant that it managed to evade some of the restrictions of the Treaty by receiving securities as payments.

Importantly to its strategy, Junkers had already developed the first new post-war German airliner as the F13, using its wartime experience in working with corrugated metal skins and cantilever wings. Indeed, as the Treaty had made it necessary for Germany to begin the design of commercial aircraft without recourse to forbidden military types, it encouraged an entirely fresh look at the subject, which pushed technology ahead and helped establish an early lead that lasted for some considerable time.

First flown on 25 June 1919, the F13 was the world's first all-metal airliner, accommodating

below

When the very advanced Junkers F13 all-metal, low-wing airliner appeared immediately after World War I, it so alarmed the Allied Commission of Control that it was temporarily banned due to its obvious military potential. Note the enclosed passenger accommodation, but the aircrew were still semi-open.

two crew and four passengers in an enclosed cabin. The aircraft's initial 160-hp Mercedes DIIIa engine gave it high performance, and overall it was far more advanced than airliners coming from other countries. Alarmed, the Allied Commission of Control put a halt to any F13 production and its possible use in Germany in view of its military potential, but gave way in 1920. In developed form, the F13 continued in production until 1932, with 322 being built, flying in Europe and as far away as China, the Middle East, and North and South America, some paradoxically even entering foreign military service.

The new company, established by Anthony Fokker still able to produce warplanes, nevertheless hurriedly designed commercial aircraft, its FII being an enlarged six-seat outgrowth of the DVIII fighter and, like the FIII that followed very soon after, was built in both the Netherlands and Germany. These entered airline service in 1920–21, many examples powered by British engines. Conversely, both Britain and France were slow to move away from the adaptation of military designs and, consequently, Britain in particular found few of its airliners in service with continental European airlines during the interwar period. At least for the first few post-war years, Germany dominated continental European commercial transport operations.

THE 1922 COLLISION AND OTHER ACCIDENTS, although fairly rare, highlighted the need to improve safety if the increasing number of commercial flights was not to herald a similar increase in fatalities. Airfields relying on oil flares and windsocks to indicate the direction and strength of the wind, and pilots being guided only by visual geographical features on the ground to assist navigation, had to be improved upon, not

below
Henry Ford personally
loads the first bag of
airmail destined for
Cleveland, at the Ford
Airport in Dearborn,
Michigan.

least if the fledgling airlines were to venture into service in poor weather conditions and at night. The establishment of emergency landing grounds along the routes of the busiest air traffic was intended to cater for the unpredictable nature of aeroplane mechanics, most particularly the engines.

Radio direction-finding by ground bases and radio links between ground and aircraft permitted some limited air traffic control, but much more was needed, and fast. In 1923 the first electric flight direction beacons were introduced, initially in the USA, while other ideas included illuminating obstructions on air routes. At airports, location beacons were employed, and approaches and boundaries were also illuminated. In due course Germany developed the Lorenz beam-following system, a forerunner of the Instrument Landing System used today, and the radio beacon air navigation system came from the USA. Radar, a British invention, came into play after World War II.

THE CARRIAGE OF AIRMAIL played a considerable part in helping establish airlines, particularly in the USA; interestingly, the US Post Office had been among the early purchasers of the Junkers F13. Incredibly, and

Typical of the large and efficient, but uninspired, airliners built in Britain for Imperial Airways in the latter 1920s was the Armstrong Whitworth Argosy, which introduced the Silver Wing first-class buffet service to Imperial's London-Paris schedule in 1927. The airliner was later used on the London to Basle sector of the first commercial air service between England and India, beginning on 30 March 1929. In 1931 Imperial opened its London to Central Africa service, with the Argosy undertaking two of the sectors, from Croydon to Athens, and then from Cairo to Mwanza. The middle Athens to Alexandria sector was flown by Calcutta flying-boat.

often overlooked, military mail had already been carried by air in France and Italy as early as 1917, with a Vienna–Kiev international service following in March 1918. By 1919 airmail services had also been established between London and Paris, in Canada, Switzerland and the USA.

Airmail was of particular importance to the future prospects of commercial aviation in America, providing the foundations upon which many great airlines eventually built their businesses, although even here it began as a military-led operation. The US Army began airmail flights on an experimental basis from May 1918. Then, a year later, an airmail service between Chicago and Cleveland became the inaugural route of the planned US Post Office transcontinental operation, which took until February 1921 to establish fully on a coast-to-coast basis. However, in an inspired move, in 1926 the transcontinental routes were given over to the commercial sector, helping establish airlines by providing regular work and income. Varney Speed Lines flew the inaugural commercial airmail services, using Swallow biplanes to link Pasco and Elko from 6 April 1926. In 1937 Varney was renamed Continental Air Lines. On 17 April 1926 Western Air Express began operating between Los Angeles and Salt Lake City, adding scheduled passenger services from 23 May over the same route. Western Air Express later became Western Airlines.

Meanwhile, on 3 March 1919 William Boeing and Edward Hubbard of Hubbard Air Service had inaugurated the first US international airmail operation between Seattle in the USA and Victoria in Canada, using a Boeing CL-4S biplane. The 3 March flight was basically a survey, but regular services by Hubbard began that October using a Boeing B-1 flying-boat. In 1925, Boeing first flew its Model 40 mailplane, specifically to meet a US Post Office Department requirement for a replacement for the de Havilland DH4 converted warplane mail carriers. Although only the single aeroplane was purchased, the improved Model 40A became Boeing's first major success in the commercial aircraft market, used by Boeing Air Transport after it had been awarded the San Francisco–Chicago sector of the transcontinental airmail service, with regular flights starting in 1927.

THE AVAILABILITY BY THE MID-1920S OF NEW HIGH-POWERED, AIR-COOLED RADIAL AERO ENGINES, with better reliability, made it possible to plan larger airliners to serve the most important routes. For example, Armstrong Whitworth produced the Argosy biplane for Imperial Airways, powered by three 385-hp Armstrong Siddeley Jaguar radials and featuring enclosed accommodation for 18–20 passengers on wicker seats. The crew remained in the open. Initially used from 1926 on flights into France, it later

below

Fokker FVIIa-3m *Josephine Ford,* crewed by Lt Cdr Richard Byrd and Floyd Bennett on the 2,575 km first aeroplane flight over the North Pole in 1926. Byrd chose a Ford 4-AT Trimotor, which he named *Floyd Bennett,* for his first flight over the South Pole in 1929.

became part of the airline's UK–India airmail service and then undertook two sectors of the Central Africa service. Similarly, the contemporary de Havilland DH66 Hercules, with three 420-hp Bristol Jupiter radials, was used from 1927 by Imperial Airways for its Cairo–Karachi service.

These large British biplanes, and those that followed, were functional rather than cutting edge, mostly suited to the particular needs of the national airline. But far more progressive designs were being built abroad. The Dutch Fokker company produced the triple-engined FVII-3m, first flown in September 1925 and originally intended for the American market. Subsequently becoming one of the most widely operated airliners in the world, FVII-3ms adopted several different types of engines, including the 220-hp Wright Whirlwind and the Armstrong Siddeley Lynx. The FVII-3m is also remembered for undertaking several historic flights, including the first flight over the North Pole in the hands of US Navy Lt Cdr Richard E. Byrd and Floyd Bennett on 9 May 1926 (FVIIa-3m *Josephine Ford*), the first true flight across the Pacific, piloted by Capt Charles Kingsford Smith and C.T.P. Ulm during 31 May and 9 June 1928 (FVIIb-3m *Southern Cross*), and much more besides.

A similar high-wing monoplane tri-motor configuration to the Fokker appeared in the USA as the Ford 4-AT Trimotor, first flown in June 1926. With three 300-hp Wright J-6 or Pratt & Whitney Wasp Junior engines, this 11-passenger classic was the first successful passenger aircraft built in that country.

In Germany, attempts to get around the restrictions of the Versailles Treaty paid dividends, eventually exploiting a reluctance on behalf of the Commission Inter-Allié to force compliance in all respects. With the nine-passenger G 23, Junkers had already produced the first all-metal, triple-engined, commercial monoplane in the world, although only nine were built in Germany and Sweden, entering service from 1925 on AB Aerotransport's Malmö–Hamburg–Amsterdam service. The G 23 had been built according to the provisions of the Treaty. However, the major production version became the more-powerful and heavier G 24, of which 56 were built from 1925, and from the G 24 was developed the K30 military bomber with gun positions and bomb racks. Strictly in breach of the Treaty, problems were avoided by allowing the

above

In a remarkable flying career lasting 18 years, Charles Kingsford Smith had many memorable exploits. Having won the Military Cross with the Royal Flying Corps during World War I, he thereafter devoted much of his life to proving that air links were possible over long distances and treacherous seas. He established around-Australia records, made a return flight between Australia and New Zealand which encompassed the first air crossing of the Tasman Sea (September 1928), flew a lightplane between England and Australia, and undertook the first flight from Australia to the USA (between 20 October and 4 November 1934). Meanwhile, in 1928 he co-founded Australian National Airways Ltd. He was knighted in 1932. In November 1934, during a new record attempt between the UK and Australia, he disappeared along with his co-pilot. What happened remained a mystery until 1937, when parts of his Lockheed Altair were discovered off the coast of Burma.

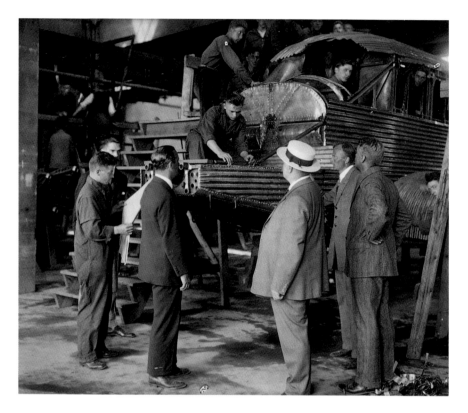

bomber to be built at foreign facilities in Russia, Sweden and Turkey as the R-42.

Among other corrugated metal-skinned aircraft produced by Junkers during this period was the gigantic four-engined and 34-passenger G 38, first flown in 1929. Although only two were constructed, both served with DLH. But more sinister had been production of the H 21 armed reconnaissance monoplane at the Junkers Fili factory near Moscow, from which some one hundred H 21s were delivered to the Red Air Force. Indeed, aircraft factories established abroad – including in Russia, Sweden and Switzerland – allowed the German manufacturers to keep pace with military development, by producing machines for foreign use, while later producing bomber prototypes under the guise of harmless civil transports to support the re-emergence of the German Luftwaffe in 1933. Foreign crew-training facilities were employed for similar purposes.

In 1932 Junkers produced the Ju 52/3m, a cantilever low-wing monoplane with triple radial engines. Accommodating 15 to 17 passengers, it became Europe's most important airliner of the 1930s. It carried more than 75 per cent of all Luft-Hansa's European air traffic, and examples were widely exported. But Germany was now in its Nazi era and by 1935 the Ju 52/3mg3e bomber variant had joined the new

above

Junkers proved particularly skilful at avoiding some of the restrictions of the Versailles Treaty imposed on German aircraft manufacturers, via the co-operation of willing foreign countries and foreign-based subsidiary companies. Here a Junkers monoplane is being constructed in Sweden.

right

The Spanish Civil War pitted the Republicans supported by Russia and others against Franco's Nationalists who received assistance from Italy and Germany. Russia alone supplied 1,409 aircraft of the 1,947 sent to help the Republicans by foreign nations, while German help for the Nationalists not only included its very latest warplanes but the so-called German 'volunteer' *Legion Condor* of air and ground crews. As well as Messerschmitt Bf 109 fighters, Junkers Ju 87 dive bombers and Dornier Do 17 bombers, Germany sent Heinkel He 111 bombers in early form, as seen here, the cross on the tail indicating its allegiance to the Nationalists.

above

In 1933 United Air Lines began
Boeing Model 247 operations, the
airline then being part of the Boeing
Air Transport System group. In 1934
the entire Boeing set-up, including its
other divisions, was reorganised,
when the independent United Air
Lines Transport Corporation was
founded. This photograph shows the
passengers in the ten-seat cabin of a
UAL Model 247 – plus stewardess –
enjoying the thermostatically
controlled heating-cooling system,
dome lighting, and personal reading
lights. Even a lavatory was provided.

Luftwaffe, and both bomber and military transport models soon saw action with the German *Legion
Condor* during the Spanish Civil War, from 1936. Thousands of Ju 52/3ms were built, mostly during World
War II, and several hundred followed post-war, including 170 built in Spain by CASA.

Meanwhile, in the USA Boeing continued its flirtation with mailplanes (among other types) and in
1930 produced its first commercial monoplane as the Model 200 *Monomail*. Capitalising on this
developmental experience, Boeing designed the Model 247 monoplane, recognised from an historical
perspective as the world's first modern-style airliner. The Model 247 first flew on 8 February 1933, by
which time 60 had been ordered for the airlines within the Boeing Air Transport System group, such was
its perceived importance. As the first twin-engined airliner able to climb on the power of a single engine
while carrying a full load, the all-metal Model 247 featured cantilever low-mounted wings, a semi-
monocoque fuselage, retractable undercarriage, fully enclosed accommodation for ten passengers and
a stewardess in a thermostatically controlled heated-cooled cabin, an on-board lavatory, and
pneumatically operated rubber de-icing boots on the wings and tail, among many other innovations.
Power was provided by two 550-hp Pratt & Whitney R-1340 Wasp radials with fixed-pitch or, later,
controllable-pitch propellers and anti-drag cowlings.

Ironically, it was the very success of the Model 247 that heralded its eventual demise. Unable to

secure acceptable delivery slots for the Boeing airliner, TWA had instead turned to the rival Douglas company, which produced the 12-seat DC-1 airliner. This remained a prototype, but the 14-seat DC-2 went into production and, by 1935, one was coming off the production line every three days. On 17 December 1935 the larger DC-3 flew for the first time, accommodating 28 seated passengers or 14 in sleeping berths. Introduced by American Airlines on its New York–Chicago route on 25 June 1936, the DC-3 subsequently became one of the greatest transports in history, with nearly 11,000 built by the end of production in 1947 for commercial and military use. Despite this setback, Boeing still had an ace up its sleeve before the outbreak of World War II, and produced the world's first pressurised airliner to enter commercial service (in 1940), as the 33-passenger Model 307 Stratoliner, first flown on 31 December 1938 and derived in part from the B-17 Flying Fortress bomber.

AIRSHIP DESIGN HAD ALSO PROGRESSED APACE DURING THE 1914–18 WAR, leading the victorious Allies to believe that the long-range and high-capacity nature of these giant craft could prove beneficial to future military and civil operations. And, with the discovery in America of inert helium gas, with none of the hazardous characteristics of hydrogen, the potential seemed boundless. The first helium-filled airship was a US Navy Goodyear C7 non-rigid 'blimp', which first flew in December 1921, but the Navy's ZR-1 *Shenandoah*, which first lifted off in September 1923, was the first rigid airship to use the new gas.

The US Navy continued modest rigid airship operations for most of the interwar period, including commissioning the USS *Akron* and *Macon* in the early 1930s to carry, air-launch and recover small numbers of Curtiss F9C-2 Sparrowhawk biplane scout-fighters. But, airship losses did occur and these included both the aircraft-carrying airships.

below

USS *Macon*, with Curtiss F9C-2 Sparrowhawk biplane fighters approaching from below to hook onto the lowered trapeze that can just be seen hanging under the airship. As with its sister airship, *Akron*, *Macon* could carry four fighters in an internal hangar. *Macon* was lost at sea on 11 February 1935.

right

The highly successful R-100, designed by Barnes Wallis of (later) bouncing bomb fame. For this airship Wallis devised his unique geodetic form of criss-cross airfame structure, which he later incorporated into the Vickers Wellesley and Wellington aeroplane bombers. Demonstrating 131 km/h on 16 January 1930, the R-100 was then the world's fastest airship.

The US Navy's most successful rigid airship was ZR-3 *Los Angeles*, built in Germany by Zeppelin as the LZ126 to Inter-Allied war reparations commission order. In a career that lasted until retirement in 1932, *Los Angeles* flew more than 300 times, including an Atlantic crossing during 12 to 14 October 1924.

With its business saved by building LZ126, Zeppelin then constructed LZ127 *Graf Zeppelin* for German operation as a commercial airship, which circumnavigated the world from 8 to 29 August 1929. During a highly successful career, LZ127 carried more than 13,100 passengers and flew over a million air miles, but was scrapped in 1940 along with LZ130 *Graf Zeppelin II* which had only been launched in 1938. Although LZ130's last official flight took place in August 1939, it actually undertook a radar spying operation over Britain thereafter.

A sister ship to LZ130 had been the LZ129 *Hindenburg*, launched in March 1934. This represented the last word in luxurious air travel, and equal attention had been paid to safety, not least as it was forced to use hydrogen gas, America refusing to sell helium to Nazi Germany. *Hindenburg* began transatlantic operations on 6 May 1936. However, exactly one year later, while approaching its moorings

at Lakehurst, New Jersey, USA, after a flight from Frankfurt, it became engulfed in flames. Incredibly, as it collapsed to the ground, it managed to keep its nose aloft long enough for all but 35 of the 97 people on board to scramble clear and survive. But, at a stroke, the tragedy blighted commercial airship travel and heralded its demise, or at least it did so for half a century. Eventually, much smaller and far less ambitious rigids bearing the Zeppelin name began to appear for commuter and passenger flying and other tasks, these modern Zeppelins using helium.

Britain too had viewed large commercial rigids as an answer to long-haul flying but, after the loss of its R-101 in France at the start of an anticipated flight from England to Egypt and India on 5 October 1930, all such activities came to an abrupt end. Caught in the political aftermath of the tragedy was the highly successful R-100 airship, which had made a double crossing of the Atlantic just months before.

By 1938, however, Boeing had flown the first of its large 74-passenger Model 314 flying-boats, intended initially for transatlantic mail and passenger services with Pan American Airways, but equally suited to transpacific operations. Other smaller flying-boats from the USA and similar aircraft from other countries had, by then, already established various long over-water air routes, making it obvious that aeroplanes, not airships, held the future for fast long-haul travel. However, the subsequent development of long-range landplanes, and the establishment of military airstrips in many far-off countries in World War II, with their potential for adaptation to post-war commercial functions, meant that the flying-boat itself was to enjoy only a short period of ascendancy.

AS HELICOPTERS CONTINUED TO CAUSE THEIR PROTAGONISTS A GREAT NUMBER OF DEVELOPMENTAL PROBLEMS, better fortune met those promoting the autogyro – a hybrid rotorcraft with an unpowered rotor to provide lift, turned by the forward force of the whole aircraft as it was driven through the air by a conventionally mounted aero-engine with propeller – such as the C4 designed by the Spaniard Juan de la Cierva. First flown in January 1923, the C4 featured the innovation of 'flapping hinges'. These hinges connected each rotor blade to the rotor head, an invention vital to the future of all types of rotorcraft and of particular importance to single-rotor machines. As Cierva had discovered, as rotor blades spun, the lift generated became unequal on each side of the rotation cycle. This was due to the speed of the advancing blades meeting the head-on airstream, thus creating much lift, compared to the retreating blades turning in the same direction as the airstream, generating less lift. So, by allowing the blades to have a small degree of freedom to move 'up and down' via the hinges, some of the additional lift could be absorbed simply in

right
Cierva Autogiros were licensed to be built in several countries, with Avro in the UK producing the greatest number. These Autogiros used conventional aeroplane fuselages with front-mounted engines, to which stub wings, special tail surfaces, and an articulated rotor and pylon were mounted. Here a Cierva C19 of 1928 is seen with Juan de la Cierva in a cockpit. In 1930, Cierva undertook a 300 flying hour Continental tour in an Avro-built C19 Mk IIA. Interestingly, a US manufacturer of Cierva Autogiros was the Pitcairn Autogiro Company, which subsequently allowed the Kellett Autogiro Company to operate its licence. The developed Kellett YG-1 of the late 1930s became the US Army's first operational rotary-winged aircraft. It seemed all roads led back to Juan de la Cierva, who first made rotary-winged flight practical.

below

The Argentinean
Marquis de Pateras
Pescara produced
several helicopters, and
was responsible for
developing successful
cyclic pitch control. A
standard feature of his
machines was their
co-axial contra-rotating
'biplane' rotors, still
used on his final
40 horsepower Salmson-
engined helicopter of
1930.

the upward movement of the advancing blades, thereby preventing unequal lift on one side of the aircraft and removing the tendency for the machine to want to flip over. By 1928 a Cierva autogyro had flown the English Channel, and autogyros provided the military with their first experience of rotary-winged aircraft in the 1930s.

Meanwhile, back in the field of helicopters, the No 3 of Argentinean Marquis de Pateras Pescara, with twin co-axial contra-rotating rotors and a tilting rotor head, became the first helicopter in the world to demonstrate successful cyclic pitch control, and on 18 April 1924 it set a new world record for helicopters by flying 736 metres in France. For No 3, the pitch of each blade was adjusted by warping, and this proved to be another means of solving the problem of unequal lift – the advancing blades automatically adopted a fine pitch angle to generate less lift than the retreating blades. In addition, pitch control could be used to dictate the direction of flight by tilting the entire rotor and, by increasing the pitch of all blades (collective pitch), vertical flight movement was also controlled. Within the future development of helicopters, both flapping hinges and cyclic pitch control would become standard features.

In May 1924 the French Oehmichen No 2 demonstrated a one-kilometre flight in a closed circuit, but this was, itself, a totally impractical flying machine. Designers still had a long way to go. Indeed, it was not until 1935–36 that the French Breguet-Dorand *Gyroplane Laboratoire* became the first truly successful helicopter, managing a speed of 80 km/h and distance of 44 km during trials. This machine had twin

below
Post World War I public aviation meetings began in Britain with a cross-country race from Hendon.

right
The German Focke-Wulf company had also produced Cierva Autogiros before stunning the world with its Fw 61, the world's first completely successful helicopter. Experience with the Fw 61 during many test and demonstration flights allowed the Focke-Achgelis company to develop new machines planned for wartime service.

below

Supermarine S.5 racing
seaplane, one of four
similar machines
prepared for the 1927
Schneider Trophy races
at Venice. With Italy
fielding three very fast
Macchi M-52s, the
competition looked likely
to be close, until all
three M-52s failed to
complete sufficient
circuits. The S.5, with
Webster at the controls,
won at 281.5 mph (435
km/h).

contra-rotating rotors. Even better was the twin-rotor German Focke-Wulf Fw 61, first flown in free flight on 26 June 1936. This proved capable of staying up for long periods and was completely controllable. Such was the confidence of its designers, the Fw 61 was allowed to give a remarkable flying demonstration inside the Berlin Deutschland-Halle in 1938.

Design of the Fw 61 had followed Focke-Wulf's licence to construct Cierva autogyros, but before its first flight development had already been taken over by the specially formed Focke-Achgelis company. Despite its excellence, the Fw 61 was structurally rather too heavy to manage a payload required for commercial exploitation. And so, instead, Focke-Achgelis developed the Fa 266 Hornisse as a six-seat machine, appearing in 1939. Making its first free flight in 1940, it was by then required as a military transport, eventually going into limited production as the Fa 223 Drache. However, Allied bombing of production factories prevented all but a very few from joining operational German units.

AVIATION AS A SPORT AND SPECTACLE gripped the world after the horrors of 1914–18, driven in part by the promise of substantial cash prizes and national prestige, but also by a newly discovered interest by sections of the public at large. In mid-1919 public aviation events in Britain restarted with a cross-country race from Hendon, while in September the first post-war Schneider Trophy Contest for internationally entered seaplanes became a fiasco due to fog. Nevertheless, the latter event, first established pre-war to promote the development of seaplanes by offering a valuable trophy plus cash prize, subsequently became a contest in which officially entered teams from various nations pushed aviation technologies to the limit. The ultimate prize was for a nation to keep the trophy outright after three consecutive wins. The 1919 event had seen an aircraft from Britain prepared by R. J. Mitchell, a young recruit to the Supermarine Company, and it was another Mitchell design that in 1931 gave Britain its third consecutive win, as the Supermarine S.6B, demonstrating an average speed of an incredible 547.305 km/h. The contest had served its purpose, and it is generally recognised as having spawned the sleek airframe lines and powerful in-line engines that were adapted by many of the new fighters of the day, including Mitchell's own Spitfire.

Other sporting events became legendary, including the US National Air Races from 1929, part of which was the famous Thompson Trophy Race in which aircraft flew at high speed around a closed circuit marked out by pylons. For the 1920 Gordon Bennett Aviation Cup Race, Dayton-Wright produced the RB Racer, the first aircraft to have a practical form of retractable undercarriage. In the same year, the first Pulitzer Trophy Race took place from New York, and many other events sprang up in several air-minded

right
Best remembered of all
US National Air Races
aircraft of the 1930s
were the two Granville
Gee Bee Super Sportster
Rs, built to have the
largest engine in the
smallest airframe. Both
the R-1 and R-2 were
eventually involved in
fatal crashes, but not
before another pilot, the
famous James Doolittle,
had recorded 473 km/h
during races in Cleveland
in September 1932.

countries. By 1934 a trans-world air race became possible, as the MacRobertson Race from England to
Australia, intended to celebrate the centenary of the founding of the State of Victoria. It was won by a
British de Havilland DH88 Comet named *Grosvenor House*, having flown more than 18,000 km in nearly
71 hours.

Along a completely different track, competitions were held soon after the Armistice to encourage
the development of cheap lightplanes for the general public and emerging air clubs, with the first in
Britain being organised in 1923 at Lympne, Kent, by the Royal Aero Club. Here, cash prizes were offered,
such as that for the longest flight by a single-seater with an engine of 750 cc or less, on one gallon of
fuel. Amazingly, two aircraft managed over 140 km. In the following year a similar competition was held
for two-seaters. More importantly for the future, in 1925 the prototype de Havilland DH60 Moth two-
seat lightplane first flew, and this little biplane revolutionised private flying in many parts of the world.

MANY OF THE COMMERCIAL AIR ROUTES THAT WERE OPENED DURING THE INTERWAR PERIOD HAD BEEN PROVED POSSIBLE BY DARING FLIGHTS OF HISTORIC IMPORTANCE, typified by the challenge to fly an aeroplane over the North Atlantic. Such endeavours were often inextricably linked with military pilots and progress, even when encouraged by commercial sponsorship.

In 1913 the *Daily Mail* newspaper in Britain had offered £10,000 for the first crossing of the North Atlantic by aeroplane, from any point in the USA or Canada to any point in Great Britain or Ireland, in 72 consecutive hours. Either direction was acceptable, and intermediate stops would only be permitted on water. To meet this challenge, American businessman Rodman Wanamaker had ordered two large *America* flying-boats from the Curtiss company, with the intention of having one make the attempt on 5 August 1914. With war in Europe beginning the day before, the flight was cancelled. However, the flying-boat design instead became the basis for the wartime Curtiss H series, which itself was further developed into the magnificent British Felixstowe flying-boat by Lt John Porte of the Royal Navy, who had been on the design team of the original *America*.

The Royal Aero Club of the UK reissued details of the North Atlantic contest in 1919, now restricted to aviators of 'non-enemy' nations. During 14–15 June, in an eventful non-stop flight lasting 16 hours and 27 minutes,, Britons Capt John Alcock and Lt Arthur Whitten Brown flew a Vickers Vimy bomber

fitted with long-range fuel tanks from St John's, Newfoundland, to Clifden, County Galway, Ireland, ending in a nose-down accident in a peat bog. In addition to winning the prize, both crew received knighthoods.

As so often happens in aviation history, the record of this epic flight gives only half the picture: in fact, a transatlantic aeroplane crossing had previously been made, although it had not fulfilled the conditions of the *Daily Mail* contest. On 8 May 1919 three US Navy/Curtiss NC flying-boats had left Rockaway, New York, on such a journey, of which NC-4 alone reached Plymouth, England, on 31 May, having made stop-overs at

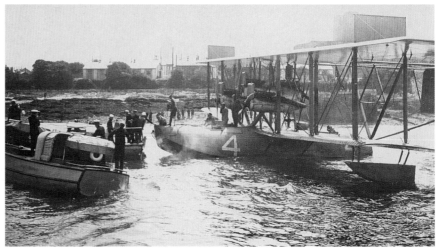

Massachusetts, Nova Scotia, Newfoundland, the Azores, Portugal and Spain. The total distance flown was 6,315 km, with the total time spent airborne calculated as 57 hours and 16 minutes. Although a remarkable achievement, it paled in comparison with Alcock and Brown's non-stop direct flight.

Another £10,000 prize (this time from the Australian government) and knighthoods were won in 1919 by the Australian brothers, Capt Ross Smith and Lt Keith Smith, for the first flight from England to Australia. Leaving London on 12 November, they accumulated 135 hours and 55 minutes in the air before reaching Darwin on 10 December. The aircraft used was another Vimy.

Many other epic flights followed, including a staged flight from Great Britain to South Africa in February–March 1920 by Lt Col Pierre van Ryneveld and Sqn Ldr Christopher Quintin Brand, a solo coast-to-coast flight across the USA in February 1921 by US Army Air Service pilot Lt William Coney, a South Atlantic staged flight by Portuguese pilots in March–June 1922, and a round-the-world flight by two US Army Douglas World Cruisers from 4 April to 28 September 1924, flying 44,340 km in an accumulated airborne time of 371 hours and 11 minutes.

above

The first flight across the Atlantic by aeroplane was made by US Navy/Curtiss NC-4 flying-boat, commanded by Lt Cdr A. C. Read. Of the other starters, NC-1 and NC-3 had to alight, with NC-1 sinking and NC-3 taxiing 320 km to safety in the Azores. The NC flying-boat had originally been designed during World War I as a long-range patrol flying-boat to counter German U-boats, but the Armistice meant that only ten were built in total, most having four 400 horsepower Liberty engines, but a few with three. The first, NC-1, is also remembered for carrying 51 passengers on a special flight in November 1918, a record for that time.

opposite
Of four US Army Air
Service Douglas World
Cruisers that began the
round-the-world attempt
in 1924, only No 2
Chicago and No 4 *New
Orleans* completed the
staged journey. The flight
included the first staged
crossing of the Pacific
Ocean and the first
staged east-west
crossing of the North
Atlantic.

right
Charles Lindbergh, not
the first to fly the
Atlantic non-stop by air
– there had been four
earlier such flights – but
the first to make the
crossing alone. His
eventful journey covered
5,810 km and made him
an instant international
superstar, also winning
him the $25,000
Raymond Orteig prize.
Just over a year later,
during 18–19 June 1928,
fellow American Amelia
Earhart became the first
woman to fly the
Atlantic, although she
was the passenger in a
Fokker F.VIIb-3m crewed
by two men. Then, on 20
May 1932, she made the
first solo flight of the
North Atlantic by a
woman, in a Lockheed
Vega.

left
Ryan NYP *Spirit of St Louis*, its over-sized fuselage fuel tank giving Lindbergh no direct forward view. Instead, he had to rely on a periscope to see ahead. With wing tanks, the total fuel capacity for the single 237 horsepower Wright J-5C Whirlwind radial engine was 1,703 litres.

Then came the greatest flight of all, when on 20–21 May 1927 Capt Charles Lindbergh, a former barnstorming and mail pilot in the USAAS reserve, made the first-ever solo non-stop crossing of the North Atlantic in the single-engined Ryan NYP *Spirit of St Louis*. Having taken off from Roosevelt Field, Long Island, New York, he landed in Paris 33 hours and 39 minutes later, instantly becoming a world-wide personality. The South Atlantic was flown non-stop in October that year by Capt Costes and Lt Cdr Le Brix in Breguet XIX *Nungesser-Coli*, from Senegal to Brazil.

A large number of epic flights continued to be made, making household names of such pilots as American Amelia Earhart (the first woman to fly the Atlantic, 18–19 June 1928) and Briton Amy Johnson (first solo flight by a woman from Britain to Australia, in May 1930), with others too numerous to mention.

IN 1933, THE YEAR WHEN AMERICAN WILEY POST HAD BECOME THE FIRST PILOT TO FLY SOLO AROUND THE WORLD, Winston Churchill gave the first of his warnings to the British parliament regarding the growth of military aviation in Germany. Both Germany and Japan withdrew from the League of Nations that year.

Hitler officially announced the existence of

Amy Johnson, British sweetheart of the air, best remembered for making the first solo flight by a woman between Great Britain and Australia during 5–24 May 1930, flying the de Havilland DH60G Gypsy Moth *Jason*, followed in 1931 by a nine day flight between England and Japan in Puss Moth *Jason II*. In 1940 she began ferrying war planes as part of Britain's Air Transport Auxiliary, but on 5 January 1941 she died when the Airspeed Oxford she was flying ran out of fuel. Attempts to rescue her from icy water failed to save her life.

above

A portent of the future came just five days before the outbreak of World War II, when the German Heinkel company flew its experimental He 178, the world's first turbojet-powered aeroplane (as seen here). Power came from a single Heinkel HeS 3b turbojet. Previously, on 20 June 1939, Heinkel had seen its He 176 fly as the world's very first specifically designed and piloted rocket-powered aeroplane, but the German General Staff paid the He 176 concept little attention. As future events would show, Heinkel lost out to Messerschmitt in the wartime development and production of the first turbojet- and rocket-powered operational aircraft.

the German Luftwaffe two years later, renouncing the Versailles Treaty and openly proclaiming a vast re-armament programme. On 26 April 1937 Luftwaffe aircraft, attached to the German *Legion Condor* supporting the Nationalists during the Spanish Civil War, carried out an extremely heavy and indiscriminate bombing raid on Guernica, seat of the country's Basque government. The resulting loss of life was dreadful, far worse than the air attack on Madrid the previous November. The future looked extremely bleak.

For Japan and the US Navy, both of which had commissioned their first aircraft carriers proper in 1922 – the *Hosho* and USS *Langley* respectively, their futures held the great naval battles of the Coral Sea and Midway, in 1942, the first naval engagements in history in which aircraft from carriers were to decide the outcome.

UP TO THE MID-1930S MOST OF THE FIGHTERS AND BOMBERS IN THE WORLD'S AIR FORCES WERE STILL FABRIC-COVERED BIPLANES, usually with open cockpits. The standard armament for fighters was then still two machine-guns. One exception was the Polish Air Force, which by 1933 had sufficient PZL P7 fighters operational to be able to claim to be the first air force in the world with only all-metal monoplane fighters in front-line service, but even these had open cockpits, fixed undercarriages and twin guns. Although Germany had signed a ten-year non-aggression pact with Poland in 1934, P-7s and improved four-gun P-11s were to be called into desperate action in 1939 against Germany.

The Soviet Union was the first to field a monoplane fighter with an enclosed cockpit and fully retractable undercarriage, as the Polikarpov I-16 Ishak, with squadron deliveries from 1934. In 1935 the German Messerschmitt Bf 109 first flew, as did the French Morane-Saulnier M-S 405, British Hawker Hurricane, and American Curtiss P-36/Hawk 75, all of modern layout and most with heavier armament. All were later to see combat in the opening phases of World War II. These were joined in 1936 by the British Supermarine Spitfire and the Japanese Nakajima Ki-27 fighters, and so it went on. Modern bombers, typified by the American Boeing B-17 Flying Fortress, were also flying by the mid-1930s.

On 22 August 1939 Hitler gave the final orders for the invasion of Poland, while in Moscow von Ribbentrop and Molotov signed a ten-year non-aggression pact on behalf of the German and Russian governments, the terms of which included the secret partition of Poland.

Unconnected with these events, on 27 August the world's first turbojet-powered aeroplane flew as the experimental Heinkel He 178. A new era of many facets was about to begin!

A Goose-step to the Atomic Age

previous spread
The tropically-equipped Supermarine Spitfire LFVIII, built by
Vickers-Armstrong, for service from 1943. With a Rolls-Royce
Merlin 61 engine, four-blade propeller and fully retractable
tailwheel, this version was operated mainly by the Desert Air
Force of the RAF in Italy and in Burma.

below
Luftwaffe Junkers
Ju 87B *Stukas* at the
start of the 1939 Polish
campaign.

AT 04.34 ON 1 SEPTEMBER 1939 Oberleutnant Bruno Dilley rolled his Ju 87B *Stuka* on its back and dived down almost vertically. Pulling out from the screaming dive he placed his 250-kg bomb squarely on the Dirschau bridge, linking Germany and Poland. It was the start of World War II.

Hitler had unleashed *Blitzkrieg* (lightning war). He believed that his mighty *Wehrmacht* (army), entirely mobile and spearheaded by *Panzer* (armour) divisions and supported by a sky darkened by the *Luftwaffe* (air force), would roll forward and crush any opposition. Polish cavalry were no match for tanks, and the obsolescent Polish aircraft were swept from the sky by hordes of Messerschmitt Bf 109 fighters. It was all over in four weeks.

On 3 September Britain and France had declared war on Germany, but thereafter did little except move most of the British Army to France. To avoid reprisals, RAF bombers – Wellingtons, Whitleys and a few Hampdens – dropped only leaflets over Germany, but no bombs. Their crews had no precise idea where they were, due to poor navigation techniques, and suffered terribly from severe weather and icing. A few Blenheim and Wellington bombers were sent to attack the German fleet at such naval bases as Sylt and the Schillig Roads. Few found their targets, and a significant proportion of their bombs failed to detonate.

Worse still, many of the bombers sent out were shot down, and on 18 December 24 Wellingtons – the RAF's latest and best bomber – were intercepted long before they reached their target; Britain had invented radar, for early warning and to detect targets in bad weather or at night, but did not realise that Germany had done the same. Messerschmitts were guided to the poorly defended bombers, and quickly shot down 12, most of the rest being damaged. From then on, almost all RAF bombing raids on Germany were at night. They were not effective, one skipper (aircraft commander) saying 'We were lost as soon as we took off'.

In April, Hitler ordered the invasion of Denmark and Norway. This triggered an ill-started campaign by the British to offer rapid assistance, which included a handful of RAF Gladiator biplane fighters based on World War I

The call to 'scramble' for an RAF fighter squadron during the Battle of Britain. A Hawker Hurricane and two Spitfires await pilots.

technology – though each now had an 840-horsepower Bristol Mercury radial engine, enclosed cockpit and four Browning machine-guns – operating from a frozen lake. Later some Hurricanes were added, but it was all in vain. On 8 June the surviving fighters from RAF Squadron Nos 46 and 263 were evacuated from Norway by the aircraft carrier HMS *Glorious*. Unescorted, the carrier was sunk by the German warships *Gneisenau* and *Scharnhorst*, with few survivors.

By this time 'the main balloon had gone up'. On 10 May *Blitzkrieg* was unleashed against Holland, Belgium and France. The French had put their faith mainly in the defensive capabilities of the Maginot line, a string of mighty fortresses along their eastern frontier. The German *Panzers* simply went through Belgium, and the Ardennes forest which had been thought impassable. The Allies were routed, and by mid-June 335,000 Allied troops (nearly all British) had been evacuated back to Britain by small boats from Dunkerque. Their tanks and equipment were left behind. Convinced the war was already nearly won, on 10 June Italy sided with Germany and declared war on Britain.

Although the British population was full of fighting spirit, many in the Government believed that Britain's position was hopeless. If Neville Chamberlain had still headed the Government, feelers would probably have been put out to come to some kind of understanding with Hitler. But, newly elected Winston Churchill said, in a stirring voice, 'We shall never surrender'. His leadership supported RAF Fighter Command in bitter air battles over southern England from July to October 1940, in what became

below
A German Junkers
Ju 52/3m transport
drops paratroopers
during the 1941
Operation Mercury
against Crete. This was
the largest German
airborne assault of
World War II.

known as the Battle of Britain. Hitler knew that the RAF had to be destroyed if an invasion was to be successful. Faced by overwhelming numbers of enemy aircraft, the RAF was, nevertheless, boosted by radar, allowing its squadrons to be scrambled as necessary and be directed to target.

It was, to quote the Duke of Wellington, 'a close-run thing'. In fact British fighter squadrons, mostly flying Hawker Hurricanes and Supermarine Spitfires and with some units manned by foreign pilots, including some who had escaped from occupied Europe, shot down 610 German Bf 109E fighters and 235 of the big Bf 110C twin-engined escort fighters, but lost 915 of their own number. To some degree this was because the shell-firing 20-mm cannon on German aircraft were more effective than the greater number of machine-guns on British fighters, lessons that were learned for later models of the Spitfire and new Hawker fighters. What redressed the balance for Britain was that the RAF had bombers as their main targets and claimed no fewer than 888, almost all of them fast twin-engined He 111s, Do 17s and Ju 88s. Aircrew losses (killed, or missing and believed killed) were 497 for the RAF and 3,089 for the Luftwaffe.

Having failed to destroy the RAF in the air and at its bases, Goering (as head of the Luftwaffe) turned much of the Luftwaffe's attention to city targets in the bid to break public morale, with London receiving its first heavy raid on 7 September 1940. Yet Britain still held firm, with an early outcome being the postponement of *Operation Sea Lion* on 17 September, Germany's planned invasion. On the night of 14–15 November nearly 500 Luftwaffe bombers attacked Coventry, guided to their target by X-Gerät radio beams.

What became known as the Night Blitz continued until late May 1941. It caused devastation to London and other British cities. At the start anti-aircraft guns and night fighters brought down almost no bombers, but primitive airborne radars were being developed which could be installed in large night fighters. The first to carry such radar were Blenheims, but by late 1940 the powerful Beaufighter was

entering service with devastating armament plus the radar. Gradually they began to score at night, and on 15 April 1941 John Cunningham — with radar operator Jimmy Rawnsley — shot down three enemy in one night. To preserve the supposed secret of radar it was announced that night-fighter pilots ate a lot of carrots, to improve night vision!

Just a week before Cunningham's hat-trick, Germany had invaded Yugoslavia and Greece. Britain sent nearly 30,000 troops, of whom half were lost, the survivors being evacuated from Greece and Crete by the end of the month. On 20 May 1941, the Luftwaffe landed 22,750 men on Crete in *Operation Mercury*, the largest airborne assault by the Luftwaffe of the war. A diversion

in the same month was a foray by the German battleship *Bismarck*. Off Greenland, this battleship fired a shell which caused the biggest British warship, HMS *Hood*, to blow up and sink, with only three survivors. Racing for a French port, on 26 May *Bismarck* was spotted by an RAF Consolidated Catalina flying-boat – a long-range aircraft purchased from the USA before the war. A lucky torpedo launched by a Fairey Swordfish, a 'stick and string' biplane with a 222-km/h top speed and open cockpits for the crew, flying from the carrier HMS *Ark Royal*, crippled the German ship's steering gear, allowing the ship eventually to be overwhelmed by British warships and sunk.

ON 22 JUNE 1941 HITLER DID WHAT MANY CONSIDERED AN ACT OF MADNESS: he invaded the Soviet Union under *Operation Barbarossa*. By nightfall the Luftwaffe had destroyed 1,811 Soviet aircraft, including 1,489 caught on the ground, for the loss of just 35 Luftwaffe machines. But this huge success was never repeated. On 7 September two British squadrons of Hawker Hurricanes

above

Pilots of a Yakovlev
Yak-9 Squadron, Red Air
Force, pose near Kharkov
having shot down 15
enemy aircraft during
11–17 May 1942 while
supporting Marshal
Timoshenko's advances
in this sector.

flew from HMS *Argus* and landed at Vaenga, near Murmansk, to help defences. However, the vast German land armies quickly decimated the Russians, and by November they were at the suburbs of Moscow. By then Russian losses had exceeded 1,613,000 soldiers and 15,877 aircraft. Other armoured thrusts reached down to the Crimea and towards the Caucasus, but the Russian winter found the Germans with neither adequate clothing, nor means of starting frozen engines.

The original Hurricanes, plus many other subsequent British and American aircraft, were given to the Russians to bolster new Lavochkin LaGG-3, Mikoyan/Gurevich MiG-3 and Yakovlev Yak-9 fighters coming from local production facilities. The Yakovlev fighters, powered by large liquid-cooled V-12 engines, and the Lavochkins, using equally large air-cooled radials, were smaller than British or American fighters and initially were made of multiple moulded veneers of wood. Later versions introduced aluminium alloys as these became available. In 1941, *Experte* Germans were shooting down Russians with ease. Over 100 German pilots gained over 100 victories each, 35 over 200 and two over 300! By 1944 nearly all had been killed, whilst the Russians had gained in experience and broken free from crippling restrictions on how they should fly. The tables were turning on Germany.

Equally, if not more, important to the eventual Russian victory was the Ilyushin Il-2 *Shturmovik* ground-attack aircraft. Despite some 1,200 being built each month for most of the war and initially suffering terrible losses because of its dangerous role of destroying enemy armour with rockets and heavy cannon, it finished the war with one of the lowest Russian attrition rates due to improvements in machine and operating tactics. Production exceeded that of all other aircraft, at 36,163.

ON THE PLEASANT MORNING OF SUNDAY 7 DECEMBER 1941 US Army radar operators in Hawaii saw their screens become filled with targets. Nobody was concerned; they must be a formation of B-17 Flying Fortress bombers expected from California, they believed. In fact they were incoming warplanes from three Japanese aircraft carriers and included Nakajima B5N torpedo bombers, Aichi D3A dive bombers and Mitsubishi A6M Zero-Sen fighters. With little opposition, they devastated the US Pacific Fleet, moored at Pearl Harbor. Fortunately for the future, the US Navy's aircraft carrier force was away from base. The following day Japanese forces attacked Hong Kong, Malaya and the Philippines. On 10 December two great warships, HMS *Prince of Wales* and *Repulse*, which had arrived at Singapore on the 2nd, were sunk by Japanese aircraft; a Japanese army advancing down the Malay peninsula captured Singapore in February.

above

In addition to American warships, the attacking Japanese carrier aircraft on 7 December 1941 had US Naval Air Station assets on Pearl Harbor as vital targets. Incredibly, in the attack on Pearl Harbor the US Navy lost more personnel than in the whole of its participation in World War I.

By April 1942 Japanese forces had captured the entire south-east of Asia and a vast area of the south-west Pacific, and Japanese bombers were attacking Darwin in Australia and Ceylon. As if this was not bad enough for the Allies, who were now fighting in several theatres of war, in February 1942 the German battle-cruisers *Scharnhorst* and *Gneisenau*, which had been under repair in France, had sailed back to Germany through the English Channel in daylight!

By mid-1942 the Allies included the British Empire, the USA, the Soviet Union, China and free forces from many European countries occupied by Germany. Despite this, so far the war had been mainly a series of disasters. Yet, on the credit side, to the astonishment of many, the Soviet Union remained undefeated and was growing stronger by the hour. The German 6th Army had been crushingly defeated at Stalingrad and from spring 1942 the invaders were inexorably pushed back. The USA – called by Churchill 'the arsenal of democracy' – was gearing up to produce far more weapons than Germany and Japan combined.

top right
Twenty-one British Swordfish raided the Italian warships in Taranto harbour in two separate attacks on 11/12 November 1940, four carrying flares to illuminate the targets, six armed with bombs and eleven with torpedoes. The devastation was terrific and, despite barrage balloon and intense anti-aircraft fire defences, only two Swordfish were lost. Here, one lost Swordfish is being recovered from the sea.

below right
A US-built Curtiss Kittyhawk Mk III of No 5 Squadron, South African Air Force, being serviced in Italy. In total, over 3,000 Kittyhawks were supplied to Commonwealth air forces.

An aspect of the war where British forces were prevailing was against the Italians. Bravely flown Fairey Swordfish biplanes had devastated an Italian fleet at Taranto harbour on the night of 11 November 1940, while British warships crippled another fleet at Cape Matapan. In Africa, Italian prisoners were numbered in their tens of thousands. Seeing this, Hitler sent an *Afrika Korps* to help his ally. Commanded by brilliant General (later Field Marshal) Erwin Rommel, the *Korps* pushed the British back to Egypt, but in November 1942 the British Eighth Army, led by Sir Bernard Montgomery, turned the tables. An advance began which continued west along the African coast until it met Allied (mainly US) forces advancing east across Algeria and Tunisia. By spring 1943 Africa was cleared of enemy forces and Allied armies were advancing across Sicily and up through Italy. In November 1943 Italy surrendered. It was just the victory the war-torn Britain needed!

THE ONLY WEAPON THAT CAME NEAR TO LOSING THE WAR FOR THE ALLIES was the U-boat (German submarine), which threatened to destroy vital Allied sea convoys carrying much-needed war supplies and food across vast tracts of open ocean. At last, in May 1943, improved methods of submarine detection coupled with long-range aircraft, such as the Consolidated Catalina and Liberator, began to reverse their fortunes and U-boat crews began to suffer the highest casualty rate of all the forces engaged in the war. In a similar way, until 1942 RAF Bomber Command had been fairly unsuccessful in its night attacks on Germany, but by 1943 new electronic navigation aids enabled targets to be found and accurately hit. For example, from 1940 RAF bombers had repeatedly attacked the vast Krupps armaments factories at Essen, in Germany's Ruhr valley. After some raids, daylight

photographic reconnaissance revealed that little damage could be seen. On average, 97 per cent of the bombs intended for Krupps were in fact dropped elsewhere in Germany. But, after electronic aids had been put to use – the most important actually being transmitters on the English coast – the bombers knew where they were and could therefore target accurately. Thus, on the night of 25 July 1943, RAF Bomber Command sent 705 heavy bombers to the giant factory. On 26 July it was a vast smoking ruin.

top
Avro Lancaster heavy
bomber of No 617
Squadron, RAF, carrying
a 'bouncing bomb' mine
devised by Barnes Wallis
for the epic attacks on
the Mohne and Eder
dams in Germany, 17
May 1943. The mine was
expected to skip over the
water and drop at the
dam to explode well
beneath the waterline,
causing maximum
damage and flooding.

bottom
Boeing B-17G Flying
Fortresses of the US 8th
Air Force in Europe,
escorted by long-range
North American P-51
Mustang fighters, setting
out on a daylight raid
over continental Europe.
Mustangs were the first
fighters with sufficient
range to accompany the
bombers all the way to
and from their targets,
helping to lower losses
to enemy action.

AT THE START OF THE WAR THE RAF's 'HEAVIES' had been the Armstrong Whitworth Whitley and Vickers Wellington, both with two engines of 1,000 horsepower. By 1943 the force's main bombers were the Shorts Stirling, Handley Page Halifax and Avro Lancaster, all with four engines of at least 1,500 horsepower. On a mission to a distant target, such as Berlin, these bombers could carry at least 3,630 kg, many times that of the earlier twins. Moreover, instead of 250-lb or 500-lb bombs which might or might not detonate, they carried (typically) a 4,000-lb 'cookie' to flatten a wide area, plus several thousand incendiaries.

While Bomber Command's night attacks began to hurt Germany seriously, the US Army Air Force built up a mighty 8th Air Force which, from its bases in Britain, sent increasingly large formations of heavy bombers against Germany by day. The principal bombers were the B-17F and B-17G variants of the Flying Fortress, with up to 14 heavy machine-guns of 0.5-inch calibre for defence. Flying in tight formations, they could put up intense fire against attacking fighters, whilst seldom failing to find the target and bomb with precision. But substantial losses were still inevitable, until vital help to daylight bomber crews came with the eventual deployment of the North American P-51 Mustang, the only fighter with the range to escort US bombers on the longest missions. Goering said 'When I saw Mustangs over Berlin I knew the war was lost'.

Meanwhile, faced with around-the-clock raids, the Luftwaffe had been forced to recall fighters from the Russian front to try to stop the American bombers, whilst at the same time building up an enormous force of radar-equipped night fighters. The latter soon noted that, while the British bombers had gun turrets firing ahead, upwards and astern, they were blind and defenceless against attack from below. Thus, many night fighters – such as the Bf 110G and Ju 88G – were fitted with upward-firing cannon. Most of the Lancasters and Halifaxes never knew what hit them, so that by the end of the war Bomber Command alone had suffered 55,573 aircrew killed.

IN 1939–40 THE GERMAN HIGH COMMAND HAD PLANNED WAR IN TERMS OF WEEKS, NOT YEARS. Incredibly, when the Polish campaign had ended, production was even tapered off, while little thought had been given to any long-term need for heavy bombers, only tactical bombers having been envisaged to support a *Blitzkrieg* attack. In contrast, Britain and the USA thought long-term. Indeed, while producing the B-17 and Consolidated B-24 Liberator at unprecedented rates – the eventual totals coming to 12,731 and (all B-24 variants) 19,203 – work still pressed ahead on even more powerful strategic bombers.

While the new Boeing B-29 Superfortress was intended to attack Japan, the even larger Convair B-36 was planned to permit Germany to be bombed from bases in North America, should Britain eventually be defeated. The B-36 was so big and complex – with six 3,500-horsepower engines driving pusher propellers, and with other innovations including six remotely controlled turrets (each with two 20-mm cannon) – that it missed the war and did not fly until August 1946. However, it later became a standard post-war US strategic bomber. The B-29, though, played a crucial part in World War II, as will be described later.

THE BRITISH INDUSTRY OVERCAME GERMAN BOMBING AND SHORTAGES OF MATERIALS AND LABOUR TO PRODUCE ESTABLISHED TYPES OF AIRCRAFT IN ENORMOUS NUMBERS. But it was left principally to the USA to introduce new technology. One notable exception to this was jet propulsion.

The turbojet engine had been conceived in 1929 by a British fighter pilot, Frank Whittle, and patented in 1930. The idea was basically simpler than the complex piston engine. Air was sucked in and compressed by a compressor, fuel was added and burned, and the resulting hot gas was allowed to escape past the blades of a turbine, which drove the compressor. The great advantage was that, while existing engines and propellers could propel aircraft at just over 640 km/h, the turbojet had no obvious upper limit. Whittle predicted that jet aircraft might eventually fly faster than sound.

Unfortunately, the British had found it hard to believe that a young RAF pilot could invent anything great, whereas when the idea was picked up in Germany six years later it was at once put to use. Just at this time, in 1936, Whittle managed to gather some friends and scrape together enough money to make a turbojet engine. He started it for the first time on 12 April 1937 as a bench-test model. Needless to say British experts were amazed and believed the idea might be worth funding. In contrast, by this time many hundreds of engineers were working on jets in Germany. The experimental German Heinkel He 178 first flew on 27 August 1939, and several German jet prototypes followed, eventually leading to production aircraft.

In addition to jets, Germany also explored rocket-powered interceptors to the designs of Alexander Lippisch, this research leading to the operational Messerschmitt Me 163B Komet which first went into action against USAAF bombers on 16 August 1944. Launched off a trolley, this small tailless interceptor was powered by a 1,700-kg static-thrust Walter liquid rocket motor, which enabled it to climb amazingly fast (to 30,000 ft in 2.5 minutes) and steeply to shoot down aircraft with two 30-mm heavy cannon, its maximum speed being an incredible 960 km/h. In practice, however, the Komet was so tricky to land on its skid that it killed many of its own pilots, often by dissolving them in concentrated acid or by explosion after a hard touchdown.

More bizarre German designs for interceptors were born out of the increasingly desperate situation in which Germany found itself, with its forces losing ground on all fronts and with heavy bombing of its homeland. Similarly, the war that raged in the Pacific gradually turned against the initially victorious Japanese. Thus, recourse was made to aircraft that were dangerous to fly, and in some cases deliberately suicidal. While the Rising Sun banner had been carried triumphantly across the Western Pacific during the early phases of the Pacific war, the A6M of the Imperial Navy, and even the Ki-43 of the Army, had found little difficulty in shooting down the motley collection of aircraft that they initially encountered. Although the A6M had two 20-mm cannon and two machine-guns, most Ki-43s had only two heavy machine-guns, but they were so light and agile that close combats tended to be one-sided. This situation was short lived, however, as the Allies became better equipped, in larger numbers.

The principal fighter of the US Navy had initially been the F4F Wildcat. This could just about hold its own against the manoeuvrable Japanese fighters, whilst being structurally stronger and having four or even six heavy 0.5-in guns. But in early 1942 its maker, Grumman, flew the first F6F Hellcat, with a 2,000-horsepower

above

Before production Messerschmitt Me 163B Komet interceptors appeared, in 1944, came prototype and pre-production 'Bs' for testing. Of six prototypes was the second, VD-EL, which was delivered to Peenemünde in spring 1942. With the rocket motor still being developed, it undertook unpowered gliding trials until, in August 1943, it made the first powered flight using a Walter HWK R II-211 motor. Here, VD-EL has 'flipped' during a trial, its detachable take-of trolley still attached to the landing skid.

right
A captured Japanese
Army Kawasaki Ki-61
Hien fighter at an airfield
on New Britain, south-
west Pacific. The
pictured aircraft was the
first of its type to fall
undamaged into
American hands. Serving
from late 1942, the Ki-61
was the first Japanese
Army fighter to
incorporate armour
protection and self-
sealing fuel tanks.

above
An RAF Hawker Typhoon Mk Ib, with four 20-mm guns.
Disappointing in its planned interceptor-fighter role from
late summer 1941, despite being the RAF's first 400-mph
fighter, the Typhoon was subsequently transformed into
an outstanding close-support aircraft, best remembered
for clearing enemy armour ahead of advancing Allied
ground forces after D-Day.

engine. The company's factory at Bethpage, New York, produced an amazing 12,275 aircraft in 30 months. They turned the tide of war in the Pacific, destroying the once-invincible Japanese air fleets.

Alongside the F6F was the Vought F4U Corsair. Originally flown in 1940, and setting a record for fighters at a level speed of over 400 mph, it took a long time to develop. The US Navy at first thought it dangerous for aircraft carrier operations, and early deliveries went to the US Marine Corps instead, going into action from February 1943. A year later Corsairs began flying from Royal Navy carriers, and this finally convinced the US Navy that the F4U was not only carrier-compatible but also an outstanding aircraft. Many experienced pilots considered it the supreme piston-engined fighter.

Grumman also produced the US Navy's chief torpedo bomber, the TBF Avenger. It played a major role in the Pacific war, but in fact by far the greater proportion of Japanese ships sunk were struck by the quite modest Douglas SBD Dauntless dive bomber. With a 1,350-horsepower engine, and a crew of two, the 5,936 SBDs built were credited with more Japanese tonnage than any other US weapon.

FROM 1942 BRITAIN BUILT UP STRENGTH, backed up by enormous US forces, until on 6 June 1944 a vast armada of ships and aircraft took an invasion force to France. It was D-Day! Important to the campaign were aircraft like the Hawker Typhoon, which with four cannon and eight rockets wiped out the German armour. The de Havilland Mosquito, initially rejected by officials who could not understand an unarmed bomber made of wood, later served in many theatres as a bomber, reconnaissance aircraft, fighter-bomber, radar-equipped night fighter and in many special roles.

As 1945 dawned the once-mighty Luftwaffe was suffering crippling shortage of fuel. German cities had been reduced to rubble by RAF and USAAF bombers, and not even the production of awesome world-beating jet aircraft, notably the Messerschmitt Me 262 fighter and Arado Ar 234 Blitz

opposite

A USAAF Douglas C-47 transport (military DC-3) drags a troop-carrying WACO CG-4 glider into the air from an airfield in Great Britain, as part of a First Allied Airborne Army assault force heading for the Netherlands, on 17 September 1944.

above

A Messerschmitt Me 262 jet fighter surrendered to US troops by its pilot at Rheinmain Airfield, near Frankfurt, Germany, 2 April 1945.

bomber/reconnaissance aircraft, could stave off defeat. Hitler had also expected much from so-called *Vergeltungs-waffen* (vengeance weapons) but, although terrifying, these were also too late. The V-1 was a cruise missile which caused substantial damage to London and other cities in the second half of 1944. The V-2 was a giant ballistic rocket, against which there was no defence, except to overrun the launch sites. One type of aircraft deployed against incoming V-1s was the new British Gloster Meteor jet fighter which, like the Me 262, became operational in July 1944, initially with 616 Squadron of the RAF. But even jets were vulnerable, and on 28 August aircraft from the USAAF's 78th Fighter Group claimed an Me 262 shot down in air combat by a piston fighter.

In the Pacific, US and Allied forces progressively pushed the Japanese back until the B-29 could bomb Japan from forward bases. Powered by four 2,200-horsepower turbosupercharged engines, and defended by remotely sighted gun turrets, the B-29 could raid the Japanese homeland from bases in India, China,

left
Gloster Meteor F Mk Is had first gone to No 616 Squadron in 1944, the RAF's first jet fighter squadron, with its first sortie to intercept a V-1 flying-bomb taking place on 27 July. F Mk Is had Welland engines, but most improved F Mk IIIs that followed soon after had more powerful Derwent engines, increased fuel capacity and rear-sliding cockpit canopies. These 616 Squadron Meteor F Mk IIIs were photographed at Lübeck in 1945.

Saipan and Guam. With its crew in pressurised comfort, the B-29 could unload clouds of incendiaries from an altitude of 9,100 m, devastating Tokyo and other cities. In desperation, the Japanese Army and Navy retaliated against Allied ships with suicide aircraft, most of them prepared from existing warplanes but with the Yokosuka MXY-7 Ohka specially designed for a one-way mission. The first Kamikaze unit was the *Shimpu* Special Attack Corps of the Imperial Japanese Navy, formed in October 1944.

Of 2,257 Kamikaze missions by Japanese aircrew during the war, only 1,321 were pressed home, with 936 aircraft returning to base (something the Ohka could not do); the first successful mission was on 25 October 1944, when five Zeros sank the escort carrier USS *St Lo* and damaged three others. The final

right
By the time Allied forces landed on Leyte, Japanese Zero-Sen fighters had become outmatched. Many thereafter carried a 250-kg bomb attached to the external fuel tank rack for use in Kamikaze attacks. In the first such attack, on 25 October 1944, Zero-Sens sank USS *St Lo* and damaged three other carriers. Here a Zero-Sen drives into USS *White Plains*, one of the other three carriers to survive the attack.

The air and ground crews of the USAAF Boeing B-29 Superfortress *Enola Gay*, after returning from their atomic mission against Hiroshima. The mission was commanded by Col Paul Tibbets Jnr, seen at the centre rear of the group wearing a shirt and cap.

Kamikaze attack took place on 15 August 1945, undertaken by seven aircraft. But such sacrifices were all to no avail. On 6 August 1945 a single B-29 named *Enola Gay* dropped an atomic bomb on Hiroshima, Japan, followed three days later by a second bomb dropped by B-29 *Bock's Car* on Nagasaki. The atomic age had arrived. Yet, despite the terrible destruction wrought, conventional bombing resumed thereafter until the Japanese signed surrender documents on 2 September 1945. Viewed in the wider context, these terrible bombs actually saved hundreds of thousands of lives, by rendering an invasion of Japan unnecessary.

Sound Barrier, Stealth
and Supercruisers

DURING THE VERY LAST DAYS OF WAR IN EUROPE, in 1945, Germany secretly loaded and despatched submarine U-234, which headed out on a long and dangerous mission to Japan, which still fought on against the Allies. Unbeknown to most of its crew, its load included containers of precious uranium oxide to help Japan make nuclear bombs for use against its enemies, plus technical papers on jet fighters, and more besides. But, during the long voyage, Germany finally capitulated. After being ordered to surrender to the Allies, U-234 gave itself up to US warships and official Japanese passengers on board committed hara-kiri. Ironically, the uranium oxide was later added to American supplies and used in the atomic bombs that were dropped on Japan. For the moment, nuclear proliferation had been contained.

WORLD WAR II HAD BY NO MEANS BEEN THE LONGEST WAR IN HISTORY, nor had it been the war with the most casualties, but it had changed the art of warfare for all time. Even ignoring the fact that that at the start army leaders thought in terms of trenches and cavalry, the two overwhelming developments were nuclear weapons and jet propulsion.

Less cataclysmic in its effect was another revolution: the near disappearance of marine aircraft. In a world now liberally provided with long paved runways, the armed seaplane in all its forms was swiftly set aside. Similarly came the equally dramatic post-war demise of passenger-carrying commercial flying-boat airliners – once the pride of major airlines operating long over-water air-routes – including converted ex-military models, even though some attempts were made to prolong their use by developing giant examples post-war. Of course, their disappearance was not total, with the Soviets in particular developing new amphibians for post-war military use for reconnaissance and anti-submarine warfare – such as the Beriev Be-12 Tchaika that was manufactured between 1963 and 1972, and which became a major weapon of the Soviet

below

Although pioneering forms of ejection seats had appeared during World War II, it was not until fast military jets became commonplace that this life-saving equipment was generally adopted as a standard fixture. The world leader in this technology became Martin-Baker, which has produced wartime fighters, but turned, post-war, to ejection seats. Here, Squadron Leader John Fifield ejects from a Gloster Meteor T Mk VII jet fighter trainer (the RAF's first such aircraft) while it speeds at 104 knots along a runway, on 3 September 1955, recording the first-ever live ejection under these conditions and also the first parachute escape from an aircraft travelling at speed on the ground.

Navy. The US Navy also took in new types, as did Japan, China and others, but these were very much the 'few' compared to the landplane 'many'.

IN 1946, THE FIRST YEAR OF PEACE, BRITAIN LED IN JET ENGINE TECHNOLOGIES, but lagged behind defeated Germany in the application of advanced aerodynamics, notably exemplified by the arrowhead-like swept wing. The advantages of swept wings for high-speed aircraft were seized upon by almost all countries except Britain, whose Labour government had rather foolishly decreed that there would be no war for ten years, so such things as entirely new military aircraft would no longer carry much importance in immediate planning.

This bewildering view was made much worse by a naïve belief that, after the losses and suffering of the war, other countries would share the same genuine wish for general demilitarisation and peace. If only it had been true.

Already, Stalin in the Soviet Union had his eye on the further international export of communism, partly through economic and military assistance to receptive nations or factions, and also by diminishing the West's role in divided post-war Germany. His long-term plans included the remote possibility of a lightning thrust west should the need arise, and various East European countries were already under Soviet influence. Moreover, many of the West's nuclear secrets were leaked to Moscow via spies and traitors, while captured German scientists and wartime technologies had been hurriedly despatched back east to assist work on Soviet programmes, while vast sums of money were ploughed into military development in general. The Soviet wartime seizure of Peenemünde, home of German rocket science, particularly gave the Soviets a head start in ballistic weapons.

In aviation terms, the capture by Russian forces of German wartime jets plus BMW and Junkers Jumo turbojet engines, among others, and their subsequent shipping back to the Soviet Union, fuelled a great deal of research into jet warplanes. For fighters, the Soviets believed the correct place for the engine was in the fuselage, not hung under the wings as with the Me 262 and British Meteor, which caused drag. In April 1946 the MiG-9 and Yak-15 jet fighter prototypes took to the air as the first Soviet true jets. But the German engines and their Soviet copies were not very powerful for such applications. Help was at hand, however, from an unexpected source.

The British Government, instead of hastening the development of swept-wing aircraft for the RAF powered by the Rolls-Royce Nene – which, with a thrust of 2,270 kg, was the most powerful turbojet engine in the world – invited a Soviet delegation to Britain. Great interest was shown in the Rolls-Royce factory, where the Nene was being constructed. Soviet delegates secretly collected samples of the metals for metallurgy testing back home by wearing special shoes that allowed shavings to become embedded into the soles. Then, to their great delight, the British Government offered the Soviets 25 completed examples of the Nene and 30 Derwent jet engines, against the strong advice of the British Air Ministry. No notice was taken. In late 1946 the first 25 production Nenes were shipped to Moscow!

The Russians had already done their best to copy the Nene, but having 25 of them sent straight from Derby was an unexpected windfall – Stalin commented, 'What fool would send us his latest jet engines?' Work was already in hand to design advanced aircraft to use this engine, and on 30 December 1947 the first MiG-15 began flight testing. Within a year it was in mass production, powered by the RD-45, a copy of the Nene.

A remarkably simple aircraft, the MiG-15 had its wings in the mid position with the main torsion box passing straight across a straight-through air duct from nose to tail. An equally dramatic development was that it incorporated German wartime research in having the wings and horizontal tail swept back at an angle of 35°, the big fin being angled even more sharply. Under the nose was a demountable tray carrying two 23-mm guns and one 37-mm. These devastating weapons made the MiG-15 the most deadly fighter in the world in the late 1940s.

IN JUNE 1948, UNDER THE PRETEXT OF VARIOUS TECHNICAL PROBLEMS, the Soviets cut all road and then rail links between West Berlin and West Germany, effectively isolating those areas of the city that had been put under Western control, in the hope of taking over the whole of Berlin. Instead, from the 26th of that month the USAF and other Western military and civil assets (plus

others later, such as the South African Air Force) began the so-called Berlin Airlift, carrying huge quantities of food and other supplies into Berlin by air. It became a truly vast operation, which kept the population supplied until the Soviets ended the blockade in May 1949, although flights continued until 30 September, by which time 2.25 million tons of goods had been airlifted.

More seriously, on 23 September 1949 the Soviet Union detonated its first atomic bomb. Then, on 25 June 1950 communist North Korean forces made a dawn crossing into South Korea, so starting the Korean War. With the South assisted by the United Nations (UN), the North's forces were pushed back until, on 1 January 1951, a new offensive against the South began, supported by 400,000 fresh Chinese troops.

The Soviets supplied MiG-15s to both North Korea and China, while Soviet pilots secretly donned Chinese uniforms and flew missions against UN forces from China, having been forbidden to speak any Russian during these missions. Their anonymity was helped by the knowledge that they had a high chance of avoiding destruction or capture, as Western politicians had forbidden UN pilots from crossing the border into China, even when in chase. As the main UN supporter of the South, the US had been flying mostly – but not exclusively – piston-engined warplanes, which were now outclassed, although a USAF Lockheed F-80C Shooting Star straight-winged jet fighter had shot down a MiG-15 on 8 November 1950 in the first-ever victory of one

jet over another. In response to the growing MiG problem, the USAF began fielding large numbers of new North American F-86 Sabres. In the meantime, the Americans offered a $100,000 reward to any defecting pilot flying a MiG-15, so anxious were they to get their hands on the machine.

The F-86 was the only other aircraft in service with sweptback wings and tail. Powered by an axial-flow General Electric J47 engine, initially of 1,814-kg thrust, it was very nearly as fast as the MiG-15, but the armament of six 0.5-in guns was less destructive than the MiG's big cannon. The MiG also possessed a better rate of climb and could take a great deal of punishment, but was outmatched in horizontal combat. So an important tactic for the MiG was to ambush high-altitude USAF bombers and escorts.

Despite this, eventually F-86s gained complete mastery over the MiGs, partly because the latter were often flown by less-experienced pilots. But, in the hands of Soviet pilots, the MiG was devastating. The top-scoring Soviet, Evgeny Pepelyayev, shot down 19 US fighters. Total production of the MiG-15 was 16,085, of which 11,073 were made in the Soviet Union, followed by 10,824 of the upgraded MiG-17.

right

The Douglas D-558-2 Skyrocket was built to investigate sweptback wings and first flew on 4 February 1948. As a full investigation was not possible on the power of turbojet engines then available, it used a bi-propellant rocket motor of 2,720-kg thrust to boost the 1,360-kg thrust Westinghouse J34 turbojet. One of three Skyrockets, with its turbojet removed, was air-dropped from a Boeing P2B-1 on 20 November 1953 and attained a speed of Mach 2.005, the first time a piloted aircraft had flown at twice the speed of sound.

below

Captain Charles 'Chuck' Yeager, the first man to fly faster than the speed of sound.

Nene engines were made in many other countries, to power such aircraft as the Grumman F9F Panther of the US Navy, an Australian version of the de Havilland Vampire and various French Vampire derivatives. De Havilland themselves had designed the small Vampire fighter around their own Goblin engine of 1,864 kg thrust, fed by wing-root inlets and exhausting through a short jetpipe, the tail being carried on twin booms fixed to the wing. This unusual formula was repeated in the Venom, which had a 2,268-kg thrust Ghost engine and thinner straight wings. It was then repeated again in the much larger DH110, with swept wings, two Rolls-Royce Avon engines and a crew of two. After a spectacular crash in 1952, the DH110 languished until it was eventually turned into the carrier-based Sea Vixen of the Royal Navy, entering service in 1959.

Like the F-86 Sabre, the DH110 was one of the first fighters able to dive faster than the speed of sound. Diving on an airshow crowd, it could plant a deafening bang as the shockwave reached the ground. On 25 May 1953 the successor to the Sabre, the North American F-100 Super Sabre, began flight testing. Test pilot George Welch won two beers from the chase pilot (the pilot of an accompanying aircraft) by exceeding the speed of sound in level flight. Making this possible were the thin wings, swept at 45°, and a big Pratt & Whitney J57 engine fitted with an afterburner (an enlarged jetpipe in which extra fuel could be burned).

FLYING FASTER THAN THE SPEED OF SOUND HAD FIRST BEEN ACHIEVED IN 1947, BY A SPECIALISED RESEARCH AIRCRAFT. It could have been managed even earlier by the straight-winged British Miles M.52, designed during the war, but the post-war British Government cancelled the M.52 and ordered that all drawings and data should be sent to the USA to assist the Bell XS-1 programme. It is doubtful that Bell needed the British input, and USAF pilot

left
The first Bell XS-1, later
known simply as X-1, in
which Yeager exceeded
the speed of sound at an
altitude of 12,800m,
after mid-air release
from a B-29.

Charles 'Chuck' Yeager reached Mach 1.04 on 14 October 1947. But, whereas the M.52 would have taken off from a runway on the power of an afterburning turbojet, the XS-1 was carried to high altitude under a B-29 bomber and used a rocket engine. Later Bell X-1 aircraft and the US Navy-sponsored turbojet/rocket-powered Douglas Skyrocket exceeded Mach 2, and in 1956 the Bell X-2 exceeded Mach 3. Then, in 1959 the air-launched and rocket-powered North American X-15 research aircraft first flew under power at the start of a long programme to gain data on heating, control and stability at extreme high speed, plus research into re-entry of the atmosphere. For such missions, it subsequently flew at a speed of Mach 6.72 and reached 107,960 m altitude, its armour skin of Inconel X nickel alloy steel allowing it to survive temperature changes of -300° to +1,200° F and, after a new coating, far greater temperature ranges.

In those heady days it seemed natural to fly ever-faster, even by production (or intended production) aircraft. In 1951 Republic Aviation, then producing the 'plank wing' (unswept) F-84 Thunderjet, and about

right
The fastest piloted
aircraft of all time –
when correctly excluding
the space shuttles – was
the North American
X-15A, seen here during
release from its B-52
motherplane. The
extreme altitude flown
also qualified the pilots
for astronaut status.

below
Convair B-36, the USAF's first strategic bomber with true intercontinental range. The 'D' variant introduced four J47 turbojets to boost power from the six piston engines, increasing over-target speed by 93 km/h, to over 700 km/h. The illustrated aircraft is an RB-36H, equipped for strategic reconnaissance.

to switch to the sweptback F-84F Thunderstreak, went into detail design on the XF-103. This was to be a fighter made of steel, 25 m long and powered by an enormous turbojet with an afterburner that could turn itself into a ramjet, cutting out the compressor and turbine. Designed to reach Mach 3.7, it was eventually realised that such a fighter was ill-conceived (among other things, it had to travel in a straight line) and it was cancelled in 1957.

Similar thinking had coloured the development of bombers. By far the most important of the first generation of USAF jet bombers, the Boeing B-47 Stratojet had six engines hung completely externally under the slender swept wing. Among its many new features were tandem undercarriage bogies under the beautifully streamlined fuselage and complete absence of defensive armament except for remotely aimed guns in the tail. Thus, while the crew of the B-29 had been typically 11 persons, the much heavier and more powerful B-47 had a crew of just three.

Of course, there were still big bombers with turrets. The pinnacle was reached in the monster Convair B-36, designed during the war to bomb Germany in the event of Britain's defeat. Powered by six very

powerful piston engines driving pusher propellers behind the wing (see chapter 7), later B-36 versions added a pair of B-47 type twin-jet pods under the outer wings. Northrop tried to compete with an incredible series of huge flying-wing bombers, various development examples starting with four pusher piston engines and finishing with eight or six jet engines, but these did not go into service.

In 1952 Boeing began testing the B-52 Stratofortress. This was in essence a much bigger B-47, powered by four pairs of larger and more economical engines (the same Pratt & Whitney J57 as in the F-100, but without the afterburner). Early B-52s had a tail gunner, but the final B-52H version, which switched to more economical TF33 turbofan engines, had a tail gun aimed from the crew compartment in the nose. Altogether Boeing built 744 of these monster bombers, and when the B-52H is finally withdrawn (possibly around 2020) it will be almost 70 years from the first B-52 flight!

In the Soviet Union the counterpart to the B-47 was the Tu-16. Roughly similar in size and capability to the USAF bomber, the Tu-16 differed in having two enormous engines buried inside the roots of the wings. It also stood high off the ground on a conventional undercarriage, making it easier to land, and

providing room underneath for a wide variety of large missiles and other loads. To counter the B-52 the Soviets developed two aircraft, both totally unlike the US aircraft. The Myasishchev M-3 and 3M were graceful aircraft with two pairs of Tu-16 type engines buried in the wing roots, and with tandem four-wheel bogie undercarriages under the fuselage. The other, the Tupolev Tu-95, puzzled Western observers because, while it had swept wings and tail, it had four pairs of contra-rotating propellers! In fact the 15,000-horsepower NK-12MV turboprop engines made it every bit as fast as the turbojet types, and enabled the big Tupolev – called *Bear* by NATO – to fly missions of seemingly incredible distance and duration. Later maritime reconnaissance and long-range anti-submarine versions were designated Tu-142. Incredibly, production of the Tu-142 lasted until 1994, by which time the same company had been through the entire production cycle of its more modern Tu-22M *Backfire* Mach 1.8 swing-wing intermediate-range bomber and was producing the Mach 2.05 Tu-160 *Blackjack* swing-wing heavy missile-carrying strategic bomber.

IN BRITAIN, WHILE METEOR AND VAMPIRE FIGHTERS HAD APPEARED IN 1943, NOT MUCH ELSE HAPPENED UNTIL IN 1949 ENGLISH ELECTRIC FLEW THE PROTOTYPE OF A TWIN-JET BOMBER, LATER NAMED CANBERRA. Small, unswept and seemingly unimpressive, it was in fact such a useful aircraft, with great high-altitude capability, that the PR.9 photo-reconnaissance version still serves in the RAF in 2003! The same design team produced the RAF's first fighter capable of supersonic speed in level flight, the swept-wing English Electric Lightning, delivered from 1959.

By the 1950s development was also proceeding on the Hawker Hunter, which eventually became an outstanding fighter-bomber, sold also to many foreign air forces. As Hawker Siddeley, the company went on to beat the world by producing an entirely successful vertical take-off and landing (VTOL) combat aircraft, the Harrier. Stemming from the experimental P1127 that first demonstrated a tethered hovering flight on 21 October 1960, followed by transitions from vertical to horizontal flight in September 1961, and then via the Kestrel development and evaluation models, the Harrier first entered RAF service with No 1 Squadron in 1969.

Meanwhile, by 1952 prototypes had been tested of three types of British V-bomber, all powered by four jet engines buried inside the roots of the wings. The Vickers Valiant had a conventional shape, and its tandem pairs of main wheels retracted outwards (electrically, like everything on the Valiant) into the wings. In 1953

below
The very first tethered hovering flight by a Hawker Siddeley P1127 experimental vertical take-off tactical fighter, on 21 October 1960. The first untethered hover took place on 19 November, with transition flights from 1961. The secret of success was its single Pegasus engine with four rotating exhaust nozzles on the fuselage sides.

Vickers began testing a Valiant with a much stronger structure, specially to fly at full power at low level. Amazingly, it was the original weak, high-altitude version that was put into production. By 1964 the development of lethal Soviet SAMs (surface-to-air missiles) had made it essential to fly at very low level. Thus, the Valiant was forced into the low-level role, for which it had not been designed, and when fatigue cracks appeared the type was grounded. By this time the Valiants had been converted to become flight-refuelling tankers, and their sudden absence crippled the RAF for months.

The other British V-bombers had unconventional shapes of wing. The Handley Page Victor had so-called 'crescent wings', sharply swept at the root but hardly swept at all at the tip. Another striking feature, which was later to become common, was a T-tail, with the tailplane on top of the fin. The Avro Vulcan was even more striking, because it had a pure delta (triangular) wing, and no horizontal tail. Later the delta shape was to be modified with kinked outboard extensions, but both Vulcan and Victor were outstanding aircraft which in 1982 played crucial roles in the Falklands campaign, when Britain went into battle over Argentina's sudden occupation of the Falkland Islands.

IN THE EARLY 1950S IT SEEMED LOGICAL TO KEEP FLYING EVER-FASTER. In 1954 Lockheed began testing the F-104 Starfighter. This stemmed from the pleas of pilots who had encountered the MiG-15 in Korea. They wanted more speed and altitude, and the F-104 gave them plenty. Dubbed 'the missile with a man in it', it had a tiny wing with about half the span of World War II fighters.

In 1956 Convair began testing the XB-58 Hustler supersonic bomber. This again sacrificed a lot to Mach 2 speed by adopting the 'minimum size' concept, with four F-104-type engines hung under razor-thin delta wings. A particularly unusual feature was a disposable underfuselage pod, which carried both fuel and weapons. In fact, neither the F-104 or B-58 was a real winner, although substantial numbers were built.

The F-104 had been one of the USAF's so-called Century Fighters – of the F-100 to F-106 series – and in the 1960s General Dynamics developed the supersonic swing-wing F-111 that was intended to replace

virtually the entire Century series in the fighter-bomber role, while the FB-111A strategic bomber variant was to replace the B-58. Although both F-111 and FB-111A joined the USAF, neither was built in the numbers originally expected. Nonetheless, after a difficult start, they became fine and much-valued aircraft, and the F-111 is remembered for introducing all-weather navigation and weapon-delivery avionics, which included the first terrain-following radar to allow automatic flying at very low altitude.

The Soviet counterpart to the B-58 was the Tu-22 (no relation to the subsequent Tu-22M *Backfire* bomber already mentioned), which served in large numbers in bomber, missile-carrier and reconnaissance roles. The Tu-22 had just two engines, one each side of the fin, but it was bigger and heavier than the four-engined B-58, and different versions served nearly 40 years, compared with 10 years for the US aircraft. The French also developed a supersonic strategic bomber as the twin Atar 9K-50-engined delta-wing Dassault Mirage IV, intended specifically to deliver a nuclear weapon. In total, 62 were delivered in the 1960s for service with the French Air Force.

The pinnacle of bomber design came with the huge (59.74-m long) North American XB-70 Valkyrie, a stainless-steel canard delta which was abandoned at the prototype stage due to policy changes. First flown in 1964, it had been designed to fly the entire mission at Mach 3. One of its other intended roles, that of strategic reconnaissance, thereafter passed to satellites, and to the Mach 3+ Lockheed SR-71 Blackbird strategic reconnaissance aircraft, the fastest aeroplane ever to go into regular service (it still holds two official world records for speed and one for altitude). Serving with the USAF from 1966 until the late 1990s, the SR-71 is generally recognised as having been the very first 'stealth' aircraft, its airframe configuration and materials helping it stay secret during very high-speed missions and at typically 24,000 m altitude, while being capable of surveying an area of 155,400 square km in an hour.

Prior to the SR-71, US strategic 'overflights' of hostile territory were undertaken by the subsonic Lockheed U-2, an extraordinary camera-platform resembling a large sailplane with a jet engine, which sought immunity from interception by flying at over 22,000 m and by shutting down its engine for long periods of gliding flight. However, on 7 May 1960 a U-2 was shot down by a Soviet surface-to-air missile, showing that a different method was needed. Nevertheless, in October 1962 the U-2 played a key role in detecting and monitoring Soviet ballistic missile sites being constructed on the island of Cuba, leading to the Cuban Missile Crisis which nearly brought nuclear confrontation between the USA and the Soviet Union but, fortunately, ended peacefully after Presidents Kennedy and Khrushchev found compromise solutions to each other's respective missile concerns.

above
The wreckage of Gary Powers' Lockheed U-2, shot down from an altitude of about 19,800 m by a surface-to-air missile near Sverdlovsk, on 7 May 1960, while on a high-altitude strategic reconnaissance flight over the Soviet Union.

below
McDonnell Douglas F-4 Phantom II fighter-bombers of the US Navy's VF-111 and VF-51 fighter squadrons from USS *Coral Sea*, attacking targets in North Vietnam.

By 1960 THE US NAVY WAS RECEIVING PRODUCTION McDONNELL F-4 PHANTOM II FIGHTERS. Powered by two J79 afterburning turbojets, as used in the single-engined F-104, this big missile-armed fighter looked striking, if not ungainly, but it was soon obvious that it far outperformed everything in the USAF, despite the handicap of having to carry equipment for catapult launch from aircraft carriers and arrested deck landings. Adopted also by the USAF, and subsequently other countries, the expected production of some 600 eventually became 5,157.

However, such production was far eclipsed by that of the various Soviet MiG fighters. The MiG-15 and 17 were followed by the Mikoyan team's answer to what had been needed in Korea: a high-performance lightweight fighter. The resulting MiG-21 matched a delta wing with a horizontal tail, and different versions added search radar and greater loads of missiles and guns. Not including considerable Chinese production, a total of 11,009 was delivered. MiG-21 was followed by the totally different swing-wing MiG-23 interceptor, of which 4,278 were built at one factory alone, and over 2,000 trainers and MiG-27 attack versions. Next came the amazing MiG-25, at Mach 2.83 (3,000 km/h) the fastest fighter and fastest bomber ever to go into service; including MiG-25R reconnaissance versions, 1,189 were delivered. A distant derivative, the MiG-31, is the most powerful fighter in service anywhere today, with two D30-F6 afterburning turbofans totalling 38 tonnes' thrust.

above
With the Sukhoi Su-27 and the MiG-29, Russia adopted radically new and brilliant aerodynamic configurations to produce fighters with extremely high manoeuvrability and capable of high angles of attack, with the blended wing/wide fuselage centre-section providing a substantial proportion of the total lifting force. The illustrated aircraft is an Su-27PD from the Gromov Flight Test Centre in Zhukovsky.

By 2003 the latest MiG in service was the MiG-29, a neat twin-jet designed to a brilliant aerodynamic shape which is also seen on a larger scale in the Sukhoi Su-27 and its derivatives. In terms of performance, manoeuvrability and agility (for example, the ability to rotate nose-up through 135° whilst holding height constant), these fighters are unrivalled. Meanwhile, since the year 2000 Sukhoi has been developing a completely new next-generation fighter.

Meanwhile, US fighter design moved on from the Phantom II to the US Navy's swing-wing F-14 Tomcat

opposite
The mighty Northrop Grumman B-2A Spirit subsonic, strategic, stealth bomber, just 21 of which were built for the USAF. A 'flying wing' that has no conventional vertical tail surfaces, control is via a series of horizontal surfaces on the saw-tooth trailing-edges of the wing. Just two crew are housed in the centre-section cockpit – the pilot and the mission commander – and armament can be over 18,145 kg of conventional or nuclear weapons. Each aircraft reportedly cost nearly a billion dollars, the most expensive in history.

and USAF's F-15 Eagle and General Dynamics F-16 Fighting Falcon. The Eagle is unusual in having a large wing with plain flaps, no spoilers and a fixed leading edge. The F-16 was launched as an inexpensive light day fighter, and was originally scorned by the USAF. However, it was further developed into a heavier and much more complex all-weather, multi-role warplane, eventually selling to the USAF in numbers far greater than the F-15, and adopted by other air forces world-wide.

IN 1936 BRITISH SCIENTIST ROBERT WATSON-WATT POINTED OUT THAT RADAR COULD DETECT AIRCRAFT, AND THAT MILITARY AIRCRAFT COULD BE DESIGNED TO MAKE THEM HARDER TO DETECT. The latter concept was virtually ignored until it was rediscovered by the USAF around 1970, with the result that what was later called 'stealth' – properly known as low observable technology – became a dominant factor in design. The first aircraft to enter service designed exclusively to the stealth doctrine, the Lockheed Martin F-117A Nighthawk, has a unique airframe made up of numerous facets, or flat faces. Strictly a light night bomber to attack high-value targets with pinpoint accuracy in dense-threat environments, it carries its weapons in an internal bay. Two non-afterburning engines are claimed to make supersonic speed possible, but the F-117A normally attacks at about Mach 0.9. The USAF received 59 full-production F-117As up to 1990, and their existence remained secret for some considerable time.

The next major stealth aircraft is equally striking. An all-wing bomber, the Northrop Grumman B-2 Spirit has precisely the same span (52.43 m) as the same company's B-35 and B-49 flying-wing bomber

above
The Lockheed Martin F-117A Nighthawk, the world's first aircraft to exploit fully stealth tech-nologies. Used for subsonic precision attacks by the USAF, its many special features include a pyramidal fuselage with angled flat-plate surfaces to dissipate radar reflections, radar-absorbing skin materials, heated air-intake grids that block radar energy, 'slot' engine exhaust nozzles to disperse efflux (specially cooled with cold air), acoustic and electromagnetic emission suppression, and much more.

above
Prototype of the
Lockheed Martin F-35
Joint Strike Fighter. The
JSF production
programme will
dominate US fighter
production for a quarter
of a century from later in
this decade.

above
The Saab-29 was the first purpose-designed Swedish jet
fighter, built around a Swedish version of the British de
Havilland Ghost turbojet engine, called the RM2. First
flown as a prototype on 1 September 1948, it received
the popular name Tunnan (barrel) because of its fuselage
shape. With four 20-mm cannon, initial J 29 As were
delivered from 1951. The final J 29F version, as
illustrated carrying air-to-air missiles, used an afterburner
on the engine to raise thrust to 2,800 kg (RM2B). Attack
versions of Tunnan were A 29s.

prototypes of 50 years earlier, but requires only a
crew of two. Certainly the most expensive aircraft
ever put into production, 21 serve with two Bomb
Wings. These supplemented the USAF's
remaining B-52s and its Rockwell B-1B Lancer
swing-wing supersonic strategic bombers that
entered service from 1985, and all three bomber
types flew operationally during the conflict in
Afghanistan and the 2003 Gulf War.

In 2003 the dramatically advanced Lockheed
Martin F-22 Raptor air-dominance fighter first
came into service. Powered by two F119 engines
of almost exactly the same thrust as those of the
MiG-31, the F-22 is naturally designed according
to stealth technology, though it is one of the
biggest-ever fighters with a wing area of 78
square m, five times that of a World War II Bf 109.
It has an internal gun, and whereas since 1950
the former Soviet Union had developed nine
species of aircraft gun, the US still uses the
20-mm M61 cannon that has been in production
in improved forms since 1953. The F-22's main
armament comprises missiles carried in three
internal bays, although in situations where
stealth qualities do not matter, up to 9,000 kg of
bombs can be hung under the wings.

Unquestionably the most important military
aircraft of the 2005-2030 era will be the Lockheed
Martin F-35. This is being developed with British participation as the F-35A long-runway version for the
USAF, the jet-lift STOVL (short take-off, vertical landing) for the US Marines, RAF and Royal Navy, and
the big-wing F-35C for US Navy carriers. The two original sponsor countries have a requirement for 3,002
aircraft, and as many more are expected to be ordered by partners and export customers.

IN WESTERN EUROPE THE ONLY COUNTRIES TO SUSTAIN NATIONAL FIGHTER PROGRAMMES HAVE BEEN FRANCE AND
SWEDEN. The former developed a succession of Mirages, leading to the twin-engined Rafale which is
currently in production in runway- and carrier-based versions. Sweden's Saab company never put a foot
wrong in developing the barrel-like J29 in the 1950s (the first western European swept-wing fighter put
into large-scale production), the big two-seat A32 attack aircraft and J32 night fighter, the incredible
'double delta' J35 Draken, the canard (foreplane) J37 Viggen and today's neat JAS39 Gripen. Britain and

Co-operation between European countries – outside of the European Union remit – has brought about the successful development of several important warplanes, including the Franco/German Alpha Jet of 1973 first flight, British/German/Italian Panavia Tornado of 1974, and French/British SEPECAT Jaguar of 1968. The latest co-operation has seen the development of the very advanced EuroFighter Typhoon by Germany, Italy, Spain and the UK, first flown in 1994.

France collaborated on the Jaguar light attack aircraft programme, the former then teaming with Germany and Italy on the swing-wing Tornado multirole aircraft, and with Germany, Italy and Spain on today's impressive EuroFighter Typhoon.

IN THE FIELD OF OCEAN PATROL the almost standard platform is the Lockheed P-3 Orion, derived from the Electra turboprop airliner of 1957. The Soviet Union produced the similar transport-derived Ilyushin Il-38, but several west European countries collaborated on the Br.1150 Atlantic, a very efficient twin-turboprop type. Britain transformed the Comet jet airliner into the outstanding Nimrod, but then 30 years later ran into almost insoluble problems trying to modify the existing aircraft into the upgraded MRA.4 version. Previously, another batch of Nimrods had been set aside for conversion into AEW.3 airborne early-warning aircraft. This again wasted time and money, showing the British Treasury that trying to do things on the cheap is a recipe for disaster. The AEW.3 versions were scrapped, and the RAF had to buy the Boeing E-3 Sentry from the USA, as used by the USAF and several other countries for the vital role of airborne early warning and control (AWACS).

Likewise, in the 1950s the RAF's heavy transport was the Hastings, with four 1,600-horsepower piston engines and a constricted steeply sloping fuselage with a side door. In contrast, the USAF was receiving the Lockheed C-130 Hercules, with four 4,000-horsepower turboprops and a pressurised cargo hold of more than twice the size and with a full-width rear ramp door through which trucks could be driven, or parachuted out. Such was the outstanding nature of the original design that even today much-developed versions of the same C-130 remain in production, while from the same factory came the strategic C-141 StarLifter and gigantic C-5 Galaxy for the USAF. The Soviets also developed a Galaxy lookalike, as the Antonov An-124 Ruslan; Antonov is now part of the aircraft industry of Ukraine. A single six-jet outgrowth

right
The Lockheed C-130 Hercules has been the backbone transport of the USAF and many other air forces around the world for over forty years. First flying as a prototype on 23 August 1954, the first production C-130A was delivered to the 463rd Troop Carrier Wing at Ardmore Air Force Base, Oklahoma, on 9 December 1956 (as seen here on delivery day). The current Hercules variant in 2003 is the C-130J.

of the An-124 was the An-225 Mriya, which became the largest aircraft in the world when first flown on 21 December 1988. It was originally built to transport the Buran space shuttle and Energia rocket components, but later undertook commercial heavy-lift operations.

IN ADDITION TO COMBAT BETWEEN JET FIGHTERS, THE KOREAN WAR OF THE EARLY 1950S ALSO BECAME THE BACKDROP FOR THE FIRST WIDESCALE USE OF HELICOPTERS, although both military and tentative commercial helicopter flying had begun some years before. Some earlier military use of helicopters has been mentioned in chapter 7, but in the commercial role a Sikorsky S-51 of Los Angeles Airways inaugurated the first scheduled helicopter service in the world in May 1947, initially carrying air mail. A British-built version of the S-51 was produced by Westland, which in military form was known as the Dragonfly. In consequence, Dragonflies were the first helicopters operated by the Royal Navy, from 1950, while in the same year RAF Dragonflies equipped a Casualty Evacuation Flight that was operated in Malaya for jungle rescue.

Meanwhile, the first-ever Type Approval Certificate for a civil helicopter had gone to the Bell Model 47, in March 1946, and it was this little helicopter that, in military form, became known as the *Korean Angel* for carrying front-line wounded UN personnel to field hospitals. Indeed, of the 23,000 persons

right
The world's largest
production aircraft
became the Ukrainian
Antonov An-124 Ruslan,
when deliveries started
to the 566th Regiment of
the Soviet Air Force at
Seshcha in 1987. In
addition to military use,
several An-124s have
found their way into
commercial operation for
very heavy lift freighting.
With a wing span of
73.3 m and weighing up
to 405,000 kg at take-off,
the aircraft can carry a
150,000 kg load.

above
United Nation personnel
carry a wounded Marine
to a medical station in
South Korea, having
been airlifted from the
front line by Bell H-13
(Model 47) 'Korean
Angel' helicopter.

evacuated by helicopters during the war, 18,000 were lifted by Model 47s. In October 1951, the US Navy formed its first ASW helicopter squadron at Key West, Florida, so inaugurating another role for helicopters.

Elsewhere, in the 1950s, France, then involved in its Algerian wars, began the experimental fitting of weapons to helicopters, aimed at suppressing ground fire. Small Sud-Est Alouette IIs were found to be particularly useful as platforms for firing small wire-guided missiles. Yet it was to be for the fighting in Vietnam in the 1960s that the greatest revolution in armed helicopters came about.

Following the French in Vietnam during the 1950s, in 1961 the USA went to the aid of the Southern government who were fighting off incursions from the communist North. Help was restricted initially to mainly training and transporting Vietnamese troops, using US Piasecki H-21 helicopters. This non-combat assistance by the US lasted until 1965, latterly using Bell UH-1 Iroquois utility/assault helicopters. However, from 1962 gun and rocket armament had been evaluated on some UH-1s under the backdrop of Vietnam, as helicopter escorts, and these trials were followed by evaluation of French SS.11 anti-armour missiles.

Full US armed commitment to help the South followed in 1965, leading to much greater use of transport and assault helicopters, and consequent losses. The susceptibility of helicopters to ground fire, however, had already been appreciated by the Bell company which, as early as 1962, had mocked up a specialised escort-attack helicopter aimed at reducing the vulnerability of the escort helicopter itself

left
Bell UH-1H Iroquois helicopters return from patrol in the jungles of Vietnam and Cambodia, escorted by a Bell AH-1G HueyCobra at the rear. After refuelling at Bu Dop Special Forces Camp, they resume operations, May 1970.

while also increasing its armament to suppress enemy fire and thereby keeping the transports safer. This, named Iroquois Warrior, was based on UH-1 components but featured just two crew in tandem cockpits in an ultra-slim fuselage. To convince critics of the benefits of the specialist type – who then merely wanted existing helicopters to be armed – in 1963 the company built and flew an inexpensive demonstrator based on the light H-13 Sioux (military Model 47), known as the Model 207 Sioux Scout.

When the Secretary of the Army subsequently increased the required speed for a future armed escort helicopter to 200 knots, it became clear to Bell that a specialised machine would definitely be needed and that the company had been on the right track. So the company used its experience to develop the Model 209 HueyCobra, based on many UH-1 components but within a completely new airframe. This helicopter, with a fuselage

above

Lockheed L-049 Constellation, one of five delivered to Aerlinte Eireann (Irish Air Lines) for Dublin-London and North Atlantic services.

frontal width of only 0.965 m, first flew in September 1965. As the AH-1G, with a nose gun turret and other armaments under stub wings, initial production helicopters began reaching the US Army in 1967 and their effect was immediate and devastating, used not only to escort but to seek out enemy armour and positions on the ground.

Eventually other, more developed versions of the AH-1 (including twin-engined) joined the US and other forces. In the 1980s the Hughes (now Boeing) AH-64 Apache joined the US Army and, although more powerful and heavier-armed, was based on the same design principles as the HueyCobra, as have been virtually all other specialised attack helicopters produced around the world.

DURING WORLD WAR II BRITAIN AND THE USA MADE A PACT NOT TO DUPLICATE EFFORTS BY THEIR RESPECTIVE AIRCRAFT INDUSTRIES. With America most heavily involved in the Pacific War, it seemed logical for that nation to take a lead over long-range transports. In any case, Lockheed and Boeing in the USA already had very large piston-engined transports under development, the former's L-049 Constellation airliner first flying in January 1943 and thereafter being commandeered on the production line as the C-69 military transport, while Boeing's C-97 first flew in November 1944 as the military Stratofreighter. Post-war, the Constellation would return to being a major commercial airliner, while a commercial variant of the Stratofreighter became the Stratocruiser, with double passenger decks for typically 81 passengers. First deliveries of Stratocruisers to Pan American took place in 1949. In addition, Douglas built upon the success of its DC-4/C-54 to develop the larger DC-6, which first flew in February 1946 as a direct rival to the Constellation.

below
de Havilland DH106 Comet I being refuelled at Farouk
Airport, Cairo, Egypt, after a flight from Khartoum where it
underwent tropical trials. The following day it established
a new international speed record for a flight between
Cairo and England, which took just 5 hours 39 minutes.

Not wanting its own industry to lose out to the USA when peace eventually returned, as early as December 1942 the British Government set up a committee to make recommendations for post-war civil transport aircraft, under the chairmanship of Lord Brabazon. Several recommendations were made, including the Type I transatlantic airliner, which first flew in September 1949 as the giant Bristol Brabazon, with eight piston engines driving four pairs of contra-rotating propellers. The second prototype was to use turboprop engines and carry 100 passengers, but the programme did not progress.

THE ACE UP THE SLEEVE FOR BRITAIN WAS ITS WORLD LEAD IN TURBINE ENGINES, (see page 161). Commercial applications were obviously for early consideration. Proposals in 1943 included a giant 105 to 220 passenger flying-boat from Saunders-Roe that could be used on a post-war direct London–New York service. Having gained initial interest from BOAC, development took far too long, however, with the prototype not flying until August 1952, on the power of ten 3,780-shaft horsepower Bristol Proteus 600 turboprop engines. Unfortunately, BOAC had by then lost interest, after realising that the flying-boat era was nearing an end. Even as a bulk-carrier for the RAF the Princess was not viewed as viable and so this programme, too, ground to a halt.

British success with turbine airliners did come, however, but with much smaller aircraft. On 16 July 1948 the Vickers Viscount first flew. Powered by four Rolls-Royce Dart turboprops, this received an Airworthiness Certificate in its initial V630 form on 28 July 1950, and on the following day was used by British European Airways on a scheduled passenger service, the first-ever by a turbine-powered airliner. Considerable international commercial success came the Viscount's way, the Type 810 seating up to 65 passengers.

Even more important was the British de Havilland DH106 Comet, first flown as a prototype turbojet-powered airliner on 27 July 1949. Of fairly small capacity, it was nevertheless a technical masterpiece, although it incorporated unknown structural weaknesses. A BOAC production Comet I, with four de Havilland Ghost 50 engines buried in the wings, inaugurated the world's first scheduled services by a turbojet airliner on 2 May 1952, carrying 36 passengers in stages between London and Johannesburg, South Africa. But on 2 May 1953 a BOAC Comet I crashed near Calcutta, with the loss of 43 lives. Further accidents led to the grounding of the entire Comet fleet in April 1954, while the causes of structural failure were investigated. By the time the much-improved and lengthened Comet 4, capable of accommodating 81 passengers (or up to 101 in subsequent Comet 4B form) went into service in 1958, Boeing had stolen its thunder with the Model 707 jetliner.

THE BOEING MODEL 707 had actually begun life as the private-venture Model 367-80, intended to be the prototype of a military tanker-transport capable of serving the new higher-speed jet warplanes then appearing. By using the Model 367 designation Boeing hoped to maintain secrecy, indicating that it was just a variant of the Stratofreighter. In fact, it could hardly have been more different. First flown on 15 July 1954, the Model 367-80 was ordered in huge quantities for the USAF under various KC-135 and C-135 designations. Meanwhile, in July 1955 Boeing received USAF clearance to produce a commercial airliner variant, which became the Model 707. The first Model 707-120 made a commercial flight in the

above

With the band of the 42nd US Army Division playing the Star Spangled Banner at Idlewild Airport, New York, 111 passengers and eleven crew board the Pan American Boeing Model 707-121 on its inaugural transatlantic jet service to Le Bourget, France, on 26 October 1958.

hands of Pan American on 26 October 1958, between New York and Paris, on the power of four JT3C-6 turbojet engines. Accommodation was for 181 passengers, and it was this carrying capacity that made the Model 707 a world beater.

Close on the heels of the Boeing jet came the French Sud-Est Aviation SE.210 Caravelle, first flown on 27 May 1955 using two Rolls-Royce Avon turbojet engines, and the Soviet Tupolev Tu-104. The Caravelle enjoyed considerable success, with 280 being built, the original Caravelle I with 80 seats entering service with Air France on its Paris–Rome–Istanbul route in May 1959. Based heavily on the Tu-16 bomber, the Tu-104 first took to the air on 15 June 1955, and went into service on Aeroflot's domestic routes in September 1956 as a 50-passenger transport (later versions accommodated up to 115). The Tu-104 so became only second to the Comet as a commercially operated turbojet airliner, although never achieving the world-wide recognition of the Model 707 or its derivatives.

IN THE LATE 1960S A COMPLETE REVOLUTION IN AIR TRANSPORTATION TOOK PLACE. On 31 December 1968 the world's first supersonic transport flew, as the Soviet Tupolev Tu-144. Then seen as a technical triumph, a

above

The first British-built
Concorde (002) lifts-off
from British Aircraft
Corporation's Filton works
at the start of its maiden
flight, on 9 April 1969,
piloted by Brian Trubshaw.
It arrived at RAF Fairford
22 minutes later.

prototype exceeded Mach 2 on 26 May 1970. But, whereas Aeroflot managed some commercial mail and freight flights from December 1975, and even some passenger services from November 1977, the Tu-144 was not a success and commercial services were quickly terminated.

It was a completely different story for the rival Anglo–French Concorde, which first flew on 2 March 1969 and began passenger services on 21 January 1976 with simultaneous flights by British Airways and Air France to Bahrain and Rio de Janeiro respectively. Unfortunately, environmental protests and ill-informed prophets-of-doom prevented substantial international interest in Concorde from maturing into delivered aircraft, resulting in just 16 of these beautiful machines being built. But these served as prestigious flagships with the national airlines of the builder nations. Indeed, Concordes proved highly successful and mostly profitable over a very long career, which did not end with the original carriers until 2003.

Another revolutionary airliner of 1960s' appearance was the Boeing 747, starting a new fashion for so-called 'wide-body' jets. Dubbed the 'Jumbo Jet' by the Press because of its immense size, it first flew on 9 February 1969 and joined Pan American on its New York–London service in January 1970. Incredibly, the 747 remains in production in the twenty-first century – although winding down. The latest version

opposite
Maiden flight of the
Boeing Model 747
'Jumbo Jet', the world's
first wide-body jet
airliner, 9 February 1969.

above
The European Airbus
Industrie organisation
was founded in 1970 by
aerospace companies
from Great Britain,
France, Germany and
Spain, proving that
European co-operation
could succeed – and
even rival major US
companies in commercial
airliner development and
production – outside of
the constraints of the
European Union. A
new-generation Airbus
Industrie airliner for the
21st century is the A380,
intended to become the
world's first very-high-
capacity 'double-deck'
long-range airliner, to
carry typically 555
passengers but with
versions planned for far
more.

incorporates all the modern advanced flight-deck electronic instrumentation that is standard nowadays allows large modern airliners to be flown by two-man flight crews, replacing the old arrays of conventional instruments and crowded cockpits.

In the USA, the Boeing name continues to be synonymous with fine commercial airliners. However, in 1970 various European interests founded Airbus Industrie, which today is neck-and-neck with Boeing for world-wide orders. Both transatlantic concerns offer a wide range of aircraft, but, after initial and feasibility studies that began in 1989, in the year 2000 Airbus launched development of an entirely new and revolutionary type of airliner, as the A3XX (now A380). With accommodation for 555 to 840 passengers, the giant will be a full 'double decker' for long-haul routes.

With this initiative going to Europe, Boeing attempted to gain new momentum by proposing the Sonic Cruiser, a high-speed airliner for 100 to 300 passengers, then envisaged to fly at Mach 0.95 or above over distances of 9,000 nautical miles or more. However, the tragic events now known as 9/11, when hijacked commercial airliners were deliberately flown into New York's Twin Towers, brought about a slump in commercial air travel and confidence in the future. This, in its own way, made Boeing review its plans, resulting in new, more-conventional proposals to meet the future needs of a cautious industry.

Meanwhile, smaller airliners developed for regional and commuter routes have come from a surprisingly varied number of countries, with Brazil's Embraer company, for example, founding a highly successful dynasty in this market.

WITH COMPANIES FROM COUNTRIES ALL AROUND THE WORLD NOW FABRICATING COMPONENTS FOR THE MAJOR MANUFACTURERS, in addition to their own domestic products, it is certain that aviation will continue to be a global industry, capable of bringing work and wealth to many. The dream of millennia – begun in legend but finally developed from a hop off the ground in 1903 into a multi-billion dollar industry in a single century – is an unrivalled story of determination and success. The twenty-first century will, no doubt, hold its own surprises!

Index

Picture credits

2–3 RAeS Library   5 The Aviation Picture Library   6–7 aviation-images.com
8–9 Hulton I Archive/Getty Images   10 The Art Archive/Musée du Louvre, Paris/Dagli Orti   11 RAeS
Library   12 akg-images   13 Ancient Art & Architecture Collection   15 RAeS Library   16 Hulton I
Archive/Getty Images   17 Air BP   18 RAeS Library   19 Mary Evans Picture Library   20 RAeS Library
21 Hulton I Archive/Getty Images   22–23 RAeS Library   24–25 Hulton I Archive/Getty Images
26–28 RAeS Library   29 Hulton I Archive/Getty Images   30–31 RAeS Library   32–33 Hulton I
Archive/Getty Images   34–36 RAeS Library   37 Hulton I Archive/Getty Images   38–41 RAeS Library
42 Philip Jarrett   43–46 RAeS Library   47(t) Philip Jarrett   47(b)–50 RAeS Library   51–52 Corbis
53 Hulton I Archive/Getty Images   54–55 RAeS Library   56–59 Hulton I Archive/Getty Images
60 RAeS Library, Courtesy of Special Collections & Archives, Wright State University   61–63 Hulton I
Archive/Getty Images   64 Corbis   65–71 RAeS Library   72–74 Hulton I Archive/Getty Images
75 RAeS Library   76(t) Hulton I Archive/Getty Images   76(b) RAeS Library   77(t) Hulton I
Archive/Getty Images   77(b) National Aviation Museum/Corbis   78–79 RAeS Library   80 Hulton-
Deutsch Collection/Corbis   81–85 RAeS Library   86 Mary Evans Picture Library   87 akg-images
88 Corbis   89 Bettmann/Corbis   90 Hulton I Archive/Getty Images   91 RAeS Library   92 Corbis
93 RAeS Library   94 The Mariners' Museum/Corbis   96 RAeS Library   97(t) The Aviation Picture
Library   97(b) RAeS Library   98–99(t) TRH Pictures   99(b)–101 RAeS Library   102–103 Hulton I
Archive/Getty Images   104–105 RAeS Library   106(t) TRH Pictures   106(b) Hulton I Archive/Getty
Images   107 RAeS Library   108 TRH Pictures   109 Hulton I Archive/Getty Images   110–115 TRH
Pictures   116–124(t) RAeS Library   124(b)–125 The Aviation Picture Library   126–127 RAeS Library
128 TRH Pictures   129 RAeS Library   130 Hulton I Archive/Getty Images   131–132(t) RAeS Library
132(b) The Aviation Picture Library   133–135 RAeS Library   136(t) TRH Pictures   136(b)–138(t) RAeS
Library   138(b) Popperfoto   139 RAeS Library   140–141 RAeS Library   142 aviation-images.com
143–145(t) TRH Pictures   145(b) aviation-images.com   146 The Aviation Picture Library
147(t) aviation-images.com   147(b)–148 The Aviation Picture Library   149–150 TRH Pictures
151 Popperfoto   152 RAeS Library   153–162 TRH Pictures   163(t) Corbis   163(b) TRH Pictures
164(t) aviation-images.com   164(b) Bettmann/Corbis   165(t) TRH Pictures   165(b) Flight Collection
166–168 TRH Pictures   169 Flight Collection   170 Hulton I Archive/Getty Images   171(t) TRH Pictures
171(b) Mark Wagner/aviation-images.com   172 aviation-images.com   173 TRH Pictures
174(t) aviation-images.com   174(b)–184 TRH Pictures   185 aviation-images.com

RAeS = Royal Aeronautical Society, London
t=top
b=bottom